Drugs, Lies, and Teenagers:

The frank reality of why kids do drugs, why current prevention practices fail, and what parents and teachers can do about it.

Alan Sharpe

ISBN 1-893471-03-9

Library of Congress Control Number: 2001089279

1. Youth drug use 2. Parenting
3. Drug abuse- prevention

Published in the United States by AYWN Publications, 23112 N.E. 22nd Street, Camas, WA 98607

Cover Design by Dennis Foster, Creative Partnership Northwest, Portland, OR

For my parents

CONTENTS

INTRODUCTION

The problems drug-affected teens and their families experience today are as real and as devastating as they ever were. As a high school and junior high teacher, a former drug abuse counselor, and a recovering drug addict, I don't need government statistics to tell me American teens are in trouble with drugs. I've experienced the humanity behind the statistics. I've seen every perspective of the damage drug abuse does to people and families—from the teenage user, the helpless abuser, and the frightened parent to the frustrated counselor, the recovering addict, and the dumbstruck community. As a user, I abused a variety of drugs including marijuana, cocaine, opium, inhalants, speed, psychedelic mushrooms, LSD, PCP, hash, and a few I can't remember. I went about as far as an addict can go without killing himself. As a teacher, I've seen many of my students in a variety of stages of abuse. As a drug abuse counselor, I've watched countless teens struggle with recovery. As a recovering addict, I've seen too many lives wasted by drugs and by the ignorance of what drug use truly means in our society.

In 1989 I had the idea to write a book about my experiences with drug abuse and my thoughts on its causes and cures. I began writing with the intention of simply putting my ideas on paper and offering them to anyone who might benefit from them. The more I wrote, though, the more I doubted the need for this type of book. Drug use was (at that time) at an all-time low according to the media, and certainly (I believed) there were enough books on the topic. I gave it up and eventually lost track of all that I'd written. Then I became an eighth grade teacher, and with shock I realized that teenage drug abuse was still very much a problem, and worse, more teens were using at younger ages. Thirteen-year-old- kids were walking into my classes stoned on inhalants and marijuana, completely oblivious to the dangerous road they were taking, and all I could do was lend them advice and information—none of which would (or could) stop their abusive behaviors. I sat in quiet agony as programs such as D.A.R.E. (Drug Abuse Resistance Education) attacked drug abuse from an angle that would not only fail but likely add to the problem.

My frustration grew during my years of teaching as I found few (if any) authorities on the topic who made sense in their diagnosis and prescription for treatment. I volunteered as a drug counselor for teenage substance abusers several nights a week at the local hospital's substance abuse program, still teaching eighth grade history during the day. I quickly became disappointed with the hospital's practices and saw serious flaws in their program, flaws that were beyond my authority to change. After seeing too many lives wasted by drug abuse, my frustration turned to action. This book is the result.

Regardless of my background, I do not claim to be an expert or an authority on the topic of teenage drug use and abuse. Expertise implies mastery, and dealing with teenage substance abuse is not a skill that can be mastered. I am not a psychologist nor do I hold a degree in counseling nor do I possess any type of credential that is recognized by the powers that deal with substance abuse. The one qualification that makes me feel confident to speak the truth as I know it are my personal experiences as a user, a teacher, a counselor and a recovering addict. I have been there and back, more than once, and because of that I will not claim to hold all the answers. It is for you—the parent, teacher, counselor or concerned adult—to decide whether my suggestions seem reasonable. They are intended to arm you with the truth before you make any decisions regarding this terribly delicate issue.

If you want help in keeping your child from drugs or if you are in fear that your child is abusing drugs, then I urge you to read this entire book, cover to cover. Picking and choosing information may create havoc in your need to understand and help. This book is not a "how to" or "step-by-step" instruction manual. It is not a dictionary of illegal substances with technical jargon few can understand. This book is not a synthetic collection of theories and research. It is a guide to help you better understand teenage drug abuse. You will learn why kids do drugs, how to discover if your child is abusing them, and what you can do about it.

My assertions and suggestions are not substantiated by any so-called expert on drug abuse or by any research studies. I write many things contrary to the "just say no" rhetoric of programs linked to Partnership for a Drug Free America and D.A.R.E. It is my belief that the conventional ways of fighting substance abuse in today's society are not just ineffective—they make matters worse through lies that play on society's fears and by submitting half-truths as fact. Give the information I offer a chance, and you will discover what I mean in saying: "Common sense is your friend, and fear is your enemy."

PART 1: WHY DO TEENS TAKE DRUGS?

My Story

My story of drug abuse is almost a cliché. I fit the stereotypical description. I was the quiet, longhaired kid with rebellion in his veins. I looked like a kid on drugs. Oftentimes, teenagers who abuse drugs don't. Most of the teens I hung around with and got high with as a teen did not fit the cliché. I share my story to give a glimpse into the world of the teenage abuser.

Who Was I?

I was a "good kid." I did what I was told, went to school without problems, and had friends. I was typical. I'd learned in first grade that smoking was very bad for your lungs and drugs made people do crazy things. When I was 10 years old I turned in a playmate who had been smoking cigarettes. I remember thinking that I had done it "for her own good." I had learned well the messages drilled into my head by "Officer Friendly" and countless elementary school teachers. But something was hindering my typical childhood. I was a bit of an oddball—a little too quiet, a little too reserved. The adults in my life could not understand it and thus did not deal with it. My symptoms of fatigue and moodiness were seen as simple laziness or mere "odd child syndrome." Much later as a young adult I learned that I had been suffering from severe clinical depression for most of my life, even as a child. This is one of a number of reasons kids use drugs.

Two Reasons the Door to Drugs is Always Open

I strongly believe the following are **two big reasons** why few children are immune to trying drugs. They are not to be confused with reasons why kids start or continue doing drugs. They are, instead, the underlying themes, or the foundation of abuse.

The first reason is the disillusionment young people suffer when they discover that trusted adults and society at large have lied to them. Kids begin to see that the world doesn't operate quite the way they've been told. The second reason is their simple inability to cope with stress and setback.

1) The Lies Children Are Told

I was an outcast at the age of 10 due to my oddities stemming from childhood depression. Once I found myself outside the mainstream I began to question it. When I say "the mainstream" I am referring to "mainstream society," or what is considered "normal" or the way we're "supposed" to act. After I began to ask questions of "mainstream society" such as "Why am I an oddball?" I saw inconsistencies in what I was told versus what I saw. Once this happened, the information I had been given by society in school, by my parents, and other adults no longer seemed valid. Simply put, I discovered that much of the information given to me as a child was fraught with half-truths. This is critical in understanding what makes kids susceptible to drugs. Let me repeat: Having discovered that the information I was given as a child about life, living, and about drugs was peppered with falsehoods, **all** information given to me by the mainstream—parents, school, public service announcements—was no longer credible, nor were those who delivered such information. Once I saw one lie, I assumed everything else I was told was a lie too; therefore, the adults who gave me the information must be liars. If this sounds like a simple-minded conclusion, it is; I was a kid. (Stay with me; this will make sense.)

Let's try an example: As children, we all went through a period of learned patriotism: "Say the pledge, show loyalty to the United States, our country is great, the founding fathers were Gods." Harmless perhaps. But as I learned the truth about our country's two hundred plus years of sanctioned slavery, theft of Native American lands, treatment of women as second-class citizens, etc., I was angry that I had been "fooled." I assumed that the truth had been hidden from me to ensure my loyalty, and I became quite the militant liberal in my early collegiate life as a result. It wasn't until late in my college career that I learned the real reasons our country is great—its ability to adapt to the needs of an ever-changing society and so on (to be explained in another book!). During those few years of lost patriotism, I was vulnerable to the bad mouthing of our country by ignorant people with an ax to grind. The result was that I bought into a bunch of extremist, ultraliberal, American hate mongering that I would later realize was junk. Think of how any other lie uncovered might affect a child's perception. That perception often turns extreme in order to mend the fences broken by the initial lie.

Look at it in a more simplistic manner. We tell kids that smoking, drinking, and drugs are bad for them. Then they see countless adults on TV, in the neighborhood, perhaps even in the home who smoke, drink, or do drugs. Why do adults do these things if they know they are so bad for them? Think about what you tell your children on a daily basis. We lie a lot—whether it be to protect them from a sometimes nightmarish society (there is a boogeyman!) or simply because it's easier than the truth (or the "look it up in the dictionary" approach). We also give plenty of false information due to our own ignorance of a subject, often speaking with the tone of an expert to hide our lack of knowledge. Sometimes we simply parrot the lies we've been told by our parents, experts, and society. Never mind the reason, you know I'm right!

To The Point:

The lies we (mainstream society) tell children to protect them, and the lies we believe as adults because we do not question so called "expert" testimony can make our children vulnerable to the enticements of drug abuse—whether your child fits the cliché or not. (Note: I am not proposing we give up Santa Claus or the Easter Bunny.)

2) Missing the Skill of Coping

Back to my story and on to the second underlying theme. I was on the outside looking in, already. I didn't fit in as I was supposed to. Why? I had no idea. I did not have the ability to understand why I was odd, nor did I possess the skills to cope with depression. This is another critical point in understanding what makes kids vulnerable to drugs. Children simply do not have the tools to cope with emotional setback. Being kids, how can they? They're new to the game of coping. Asking a 4-year-old to cope with the stress of having a new baby sister is like asking him to perform a back flip. He hasn't had time to practice and acquire the new skills (like sharing or understanding jealousy) necessary to get along with a new sibling. Emotional skills are no different from other categories of skills in that they must be learned and practiced. Ask a baker to deal with the politics of being a senator and that baker will likely freeze with indecision. Ask a senator to bake a thousand loaves of bread and you'll get a mess. Emotional undertakings are no different. Dealing with emotions requires certain skills that can only be learned through experience and thoughtful reflection—*reflection* being another skill kids don't generally have. Physical skills (balancing, walking, riding a bike) and thinking skills (problem solving, critical thinking), are NO DIFFERENT from emotional skills (coping with loss, tragedy, stress) in that mastering them takes TIME.

Reacting to setback is relatively easy for an adult. We've had them before, some worse than others. Most of us can "pick ourselves up" and try again. But to a child, every setback has a new set of rules in dealing with it, requiring the use of a new mixture of emotional safeguards and reactions (or skills). As a child, I did not know how to pick myself up after a setback. Most kids don't. They do their best to muddle through. Whether the setback is a poor grade or losing a mitten in the snow, a child will react with a typical pout if he or she doesn't understand how to cope with such minor crises. Do we as teachers, parents, and members of our community teach children that for every one success there may be a hundred failures? Do we **actively** teach them the skills of coping, or is it more of a "learn as you go" method? Don't agree too quickly without seeing the dangerous flip side. The psychological trick here is that teaching coping skills is not the same as setting children up for failure by bracing them for it (the "don't be disappointed if it doesn't work out" method).

To The Point:

Kids are not equipped with the skills of coping, and they have far more to cope with than previous generations. This lack of skills makes them vulnerable to alternative means of coping with stress—such as drugs.

Why Teens Turn to Drugs

Nearly all children are lied to and nearly all have yet to master the skills of coping. Is that why I turned to drugs? Why then don't all children? I wish I could give you the pamphlet version that most drug abuse prevention groups hand out by the thousands, but it is simply not that simple. With that in mind, please read this section at least twice. Understand it, and then weigh it against what you know. If it makes sense, we can go forward. If not, the rest of this book becomes largely useless to you. Please recycle if this is the case.

Disillusionment

I became an outcast because my clinical depression made me an odd child. I spent a lot of time alone and became very introspective. Wasn't *introspection* a skill I needed? Yes, but I had no guidance in my self-questioning and self-analysis (sometimes poor skills are worse than no skills.) I thought about what was going on inside me more than most of my peers. I tossed around the same questions over and over. I did not move forward. I was a dweller and I often dwelled on the question: Why am I different? I was sad and upset for no reason. Kids don't like to play ball with a child who's quiet. On top of it, I lived in the shadow of two star brothers. My parents never had to say, "Why can't you be like your brother?" because I thought it on my own. Why were they stars and I was not? I thought it was my fault. I had failed somehow. What other conclusion could a child reach? *Rational thinking* was not something I'd learned yet. My brothers were indeed stars—no sarcasm intended. One was a National Honor Society mega-brain and the other a budding young star athlete that all the girls loved. My parents bounded with pride about their star children. As for me, my weird kid behavior was just plain confusing to them. Speaking of skills, they didn't know how to deal with me, and no one was there to help them. This was long before depression was understood or even recognized as an illness.

My oddities found no home, no comfort, and no place where they could be accepted until I discovered the drug culture. I was in seventh grade—13 years old—when a kid I went to school with presented a question: Had I ever smoked dope (marijuana)? Of course I hadn't. **Why would I try?** Especially after buying into the "drugs are bad" speeches I had heard in elementary school (later to be called the "Just say no" campaign).

I grew up with a set of values placed upon me that were understandably well intentioned. Regardless of the reasons why, I discovered that many of those values where flawed—just like the lies we tell our kids. Just one of a hundred examples: I was told by parents, teachers, TV, radio and billboards that if I set my mind to a task, I could do anything. If I tried hard, I'd be good. I tried hard to be a good baseball player, yet I had problems throwing the ball to first base (I played second base). As a child I thought that it was my fault for not living up to expectations. No one (parents, teachers, coaches and the like) understood that horrible pressure to perform and succeed (as society said I was supposed to) nor the damage my shortcomings did to my fragile 10-year-old psyche (as most 10-year-old psyches are). I didn't and couldn't understand it at that time. I thought, "Aren't they (adults) supposed to understand? All adults understand what kids go through and they are there to help, right?" Yet another half-truth we tell kids. Honestly, there are many adults out there who don't understand their own problems let alone those of a 10-year-old. And of course, some adults deal with their problems *like* 10-year-olds.

I began to see the ambiguities and shortcomings of what "mainstream society" was preaching to me. My friend wanted me to try marijuana. I had been told drugs were bad. Perhaps, too, the words of warning about drugs were flawed or just flat out lies. My growing disillusionment broke down the false barrier that had been established in elementary school.

Curiosity

Besides being a seemingly basic behavior to most animals, curiosity is often taught to our children as being a valuable learning tool. We urge and encourage them to question and use curiosity to explore the world around them. We then expect them to ignore those lessons for anything we deem as being dangerous or destructive. It was that inherent and learned curiosity that made me want to try marijuana. Peer pressure –the biggest cop-out we allow children to use—had nothing to do with my willingness to try drugs. I was curious and that curiosity no longer had barriers to prevent me from acting on it. If adults were supposed to be helpful yet weren't, if I was supposed to succeed if I tried hard and didn't, perhaps drugs weren't the demon monster I was told they were. After all, I had met kids in school who did drugs and were on drugs. They weren't out-of-control, lunatic monsters or horribly desolate souls like all the anti-drug posters and TV commercials depicted. They were just kids, kids who seemed to have a better handle on life than I did. I was curious why that was, and the fear instilled in me by the mainstream no longer seemed valid. They'd already been proven liars. This is what I mean when I say I became disillusioned. I saw the forest for the trees, and I was curious as to what was in those woods.

Experimentation

Despite our best efforts to protect our children, they learn best through trial and error. Think of how often you were told as a child that the stove or a candle is hot: "Don't touch it." I'd probably be right in guessing that as a child you were burned by touching a hot stove. You were curious and decided to see for yourself. Experimentation is curiosity acted upon. When I was a teen I knew several teens who had experimented with marijuana once or twice, did not like it, and that was the end of it; their curiosity had been satisfied. I also knew kids who had became weekend smokers for a few months, then the "thrill" faded and they gave up the practice. Not every child who tries drugs becomes an addict. Many who are curious and experiment, do.

The Hook of Drugs

My 13-year-old friend (the one who asked if I had ever tried marijuana) and I walked to the park after school one day and smoked a joint (a marijuana cigarette). I didn't hesitate. I choked on the thick marijuana smoke as any young smoker of a cigarette would but did my best to hold the "hit" in my lungs for as long as possible. Soon after, I began to experience an altered reality, feeling somewhat like someone who is coming down with the flu might feel. The difference was that it felt good. A euphoric feeling of greatness and possibility came over me. It was wonderful. The hook had found its mark. Once I "got high" for the first time, a door opened up. Marijuana made me feel good, confident, and able. I was happy, I laughed, the air seemed sweet, and food tasted absolutely delicious. It was truly the best feeling I'd ever felt in my short 13-year-old life (Of course, to a 13-year-old, today and yesterday are what's most important—not tomorrow).

Pay special attention to this: One of the most dangerous attributes of drugs is that hook. Here is the problem: The dangerous nature of marijuana (which we have yet to cover) gets caught in the lies and half-truths children are told about it. The child asks, "How can something that makes one feel so good be considered to be so dangerous by adults?" I wasn't becoming an idiotic monster. I felt alive. I felt confident. And most importantly, I no longer felt any of the pressure and stress of being a kid. I didn't have to try to cope or use skills I had yet to develop. Coping became automatic. I was the best person I'd ever been (so I thought). I questioned myself, "How can this be bad? How can it be wrong?" I had been lied to again. The "Just say no" rhetoric was too superficial and had in a small way helped deliver me to drug use. From that day forward, little of what any adult told me from a moral point of view did I trust to be true. For that ounce of marijuana-induced elation, though, I'd experience megatons of torture.

It could be argued that it was simple bad luck that I met a kid who did drugs and I followed the path I did. It could be argued that I might have found another outlet to deal with my depression. But that would ignore the fact that escape from any exposure to drugs is impossible for children growing up in this era. It is everywhere.

To The Point:

Disillusionment, curiosity and experimentation lead to poor choices. The opportunity to make those choices is enhanced by people who preach and parrot pale anti-drug messages and thus provide a false image of drug abuse. Once a teen tries drugs and sees those images to be false due to the "hook" or the euphoric feelings, he or she is lost. We will soon discuss the true horrors of drug abuse.

Pressure: "Good Kids" Do Drugs, Too

I was a good kid. I came from a seemingly solid family: two parents, a good home, no physical abuse whatsoever, my parents and two brothers were respected in the community, etc. My parents were successful in instilling in me a set of core values (separate from statements of morality) that I rarely ignored. I was polite to adults, I stayed out of trouble at school, and I didn't steal—well, on a few occasions. Regardless, I looked like a kid on drugs. I looked like a "bad kid." I fit the profile from head to toe: long hair, flannel shirts, blue jeans, rock T-shirts, worn face, and bloodshot eyes. So, what about the kids who don't fit that cliché? What about the kids who look like mainstream society wants them to look, act like they are supposed to act, and get good grades as well? Why do they get hooked? The same reasons I did. I could take as examples a dozen kids I knew as a teen who were from middle-class to upper-class backgrounds, had both parents in the home who were seemingly loving and caring, had a nurturing community and extended family relationships, played sports, dated all the pretty people, had a dog, but abused drugs worse than I did. Why? The pressures of living, the lies of society, and the inability to cope with those pressures and lies.

I was under the pressure and strain of depression and

being an outcast. I did not have the skills to deal with that properly, and I easily fell in with a crowd that accepted me. I saw the half-truths for what they were. The "good-kids" had pressures too. And perhaps far more lies to live up to, subtle, hidden, and far more dangerous. The mainstream (parents, teachers, society, even the nature of our culture) creates goals for our children that are sometimes—if not often—unattainable, when taken individually. To achieve them all at once though is outrageous: get good grades, have the right friends, participate in the right activities, look towards college, do what you are told while creating a sense of individuality, achieve, achieve, achieve and if you can't, you've failed. No one ever says this outright, but it is the message. Do I need to explain this one, or do you see this as being as obvious as I do?

Competition is placed at the heart of attaining those goals. Everywhere we turn, from family and friends to television and advertising, kids are told: "You can be anything you want to be," "You can do anything you set your mind to do," "You can be the best," "You can achieve more than those who came before you," "You can do better than your parents." "Even if you can't," comes the implication, "certainly you can keep up with the crowd of children trying do as you are trying to do." Is any of that true? For every one person who became everything he or she wanted to be, how many didn't make it? Lack of ability, raw talent, coaching, simple knowledge—there are a hundred reasons for failure, and failure is devastating to a child who lives in a success-driven society. Any one of those failures can grab a kid at any time and make him or her vulnerable. I truly believe that the more prosperous our country becomes, the higher the expectations for our children become. I was lucky; I had already given up and did not have to meet any expectations. Many of my friends (the "good kids"), however, had to endure that pressure for their entire youth while maintaining a convincing front.

To The Point:

Re-read the last paragraph and ask yourself: "Does this make sense?" "Does society do this to our children?" Half-truths told to children combined with their lack of coping skills bring on disillusionment, curiosity, experimentation, and intense pressure to open the door to experiencing the hook of drugs. It is too simple-minded to say that kids do drugs because they think it's cool or because of peer pressure.

The Culturally Embedded

These explanations are certainly not a catchall for why all kids begin using drugs. There are many people who use drugs because it is part of the culture in which they grew up. Perhaps Mom and Dad use drugs or a friend's parents or big brothers and sisters or next-door neighbors or all of those mentioned are users. Unfortunately, these conditions exist in our nation today with a frequency that discounts them as rare occurrences. These cultures crop up everywhere from urban centers to rural communities. The use of illegal substances is accepted as a way of life in these cultures, and the idea has been passed down through generations. Regardless of how the custom was started, it is forwarded through the belief that drug use is no different from alcohol use (a fact which is indeed hard to debate) with the "minor" difference being the illegality of the former. As a teen, having friends from this culture helped me rationalize my newfound assumption that drug use was OK. As a sidebar, I had some friends who grew up drug-free in this culture though their parents were pot smokers. No rules are concrete here.

A community with drug use embedded as the norm

is comparable to alcohol consumption of the late 70's and early 80's before awareness reached a wide audience. Drinking was OK, a victimless crime for teens who were simply spreading their wings. Many parents threw parties for their teenager's graduation allowing and even purchasing alcohol for the enjoyment of the young partygoers. Television and other public outlets for media showed alcohol consumption as part of the American Way or a rite of passage (this still happens to a large extent today). Often parents passively condone underage drinking with older teens as long as they don't drink and drive. Today with the horrible failure of the so-called "War on Drugs" and the anti-drug rhetoric added to the emergence of an American society that looks at marijuana use as relatively harmless (often glamorizing its use in TV and film), the growth of such cultures where drug use is the norm will increase.

Depression

I was suffering (and still do though treated) from severe clinical depression, which results from a chemical imbalance in the brain. Depression is an illness as real as cancer and as potentially deadly. Clinical depression is not a simple case of the blues. It is a medical condition that cannot be helped nor controlled by the individual without medical intervention. This illness has become more understood through the years but still remains a taboo topic for many people and is looked at as being a "made-up" illness. Because it is so hard to understand, the illness often goes untreated. In my case, I thought something was wrong with me. I felt it was my fault and therefore I could correct it. In trying to correct it I self-medicated with illegal drugs, somehow thinking it would buy me time until I "snapped out of it." I did not know that a person could not and cannot "snap out" of clinical depression. In order to avoid dealing with a serious condition that I saw as something I should be able to control, I gladly took and continued to take the temporary out of drugs. In brief, some teens turn to drugs to deal with depression or any other serious mental illness.

Summary

In short, this is why I believe teens do drugs:

1. A foundation is set for most children, which makes them vulnerable to trying drugs.
    - **The Lies:**
      We actively lie to our children for a variety of good and bad reasons. Eventually these lies are discovered and the bonds of trust are broken.
    - **The Skills of Coping:**
      We do not actively teach children the skills of coping with daily stress and setbacks, both of which are far more intense for today's kids then those who came before them.

2. After the foundation is set, kids can turn to drugs for a variety of reasons.
    - **Disillusionment:**
      Kids are smart. Once they see one statement of wrong and right disproved, they question every statement whether correct or not.
    - **Curiosity:**
      Kids are curious by nature. With the foundation in place, that curiosity has few barriers.
    - **Experimentation:**
      This takes place when kids act on their curiosity. It doesn't always lead to drug abuse but should not be ignored.
    - **The Hook:**

Drugs do enhance the pleasure zones of the brain. The true evil of drugs (soon to be discussed) is that the user cannot easily identify their dangers.

- **Pressure:**

Everyone is at risk. Stress and pressure know no social or cultural barriers.

- **A Drug Culture:**

Some kids turn to drugs because they've grown up in a culture that approves of them.

- **Depression:**

Sometimes medical reasons can lead to a child's use of illegal drugs.

Why Teens Become Addicts

Reinventing Myself

By the time I was in eighth grade I was a weekend addict. My friends and I would go ice skating every Friday and Saturday and then, having a 10 or 11 p.m. curfew to "go to the pizza place after skating," we'd make a 9 p.m. trip to the golf course to smoke marijuana. It was a great experience—or so I thought. I had friends with a common interest. If I had dope, I became instantly (and temporarily) popular with those who wanted it. Kids came to me to talk because I shared their disillusionment and I shared my drugs. We swapped stories of the "horrible injustices" our parents, teachers, and other adults had delivered to us. It became a bizarre unintended contest at times: Whose parents were worse? Who had the most pain to endure? We wore the injustices like battle scars. They gave us purpose.

I remember hearing a rather obtuse phrase growing up: "A friend with weed is a friend indeed." By the time

I was in high school, I had many "friends." I could get dope with a simple phone call and was supporting my daily habit by selling joints. Little did I know that I'd started on a path of smoking marijuana every day of my life that would last for six years. As I smoked more, I did less. I had played sports since fifth grade: track, soccer, and hockey. By my senior year I wasn't active in anything. As a sophomore I began getting high before school (we called it "wake-and-bake"), immediately after school, and at night. I was too afraid to get high during school. My friends weren't, and many got caught. The law did not scare me; my parents did not scare me; the thought of being caught and not being able to get high scared me. I had found a tool to cope with setback. The problem was that the tool was illegal, dangerous, and very misleading, for it only hid the pain of failure. I never actually had to deal with failure.

The Next Level

I had become a pro at using drugs and coping with life through drugs by the age of 15. I could identify different types of marijuana and eyeball-measure amounts in a plastic bag to determine their weight and value. I could roll a bag of marijuana into joints in ten minutes, extracting seeds and stems (which are not smokable) as I worked. I got high with ease in my bedroom while my parents watched the nightly news. I hid the smell of smoke from the burning weed with a "sneak-a-toke" or a "one-hitter." I hid the smell of exhaled marijuana with a simple method: blowing the smoke through a used paper towel roll stuffed with fabric softener sheets.

I took it up several notches the summer after my sophomore year. Having access to a car gave me options I could not have otherwise pursued. I was using inhalants (huffing) and taking amphetamines (speed). I'd tried cocaine, LSD, PCP, a host of other drugs, and even tried smoking a dried banana peel having heard it had psychotropic properties (It just made me sick). Cocaine would become my next conquest. After smoking as much marijuana as I had smoked, the effects became less pronounced. Happiness was not achieved with one toke ("toke" meaning to inhale), or even several. I'd still get high but it wasn't providing the fun it used to. Once users have experienced that euphoria, they want it again, and when marijuana fails to provide it, they turn to harder drugs. Because of this, marijuana is often referred to as a "gateway drug."

I was hooked on cocaine in a classic manner. An older friend would call me up to go out on a Friday or Saturday night. I was in awe of the fact an older guy wanted to be my friend, so I was always eager to hang out with him. We'd go to parties where all the older cool kids hung out, and he'd give me enough free coke to *almost* satisfy me. He'd drop me off at home late in the evening knowing I wanted more. Then one night, he simply said: "Hey man, this stuff's not free, you know. I can't just keep giving it to you." Money began to disappear from my savings account, and any cash given to me by my parents to go out with friends was spent on coke, marijuana, and alcohol. I always had an excuse as to why I needed the money. I always found a way to get money without stealing, although I did turn to that on a few occasions. Besides, I was still selling marijuana to help support my habits. By this time I had dope smoking, coke sniffing, booze drinking friends who were from all backgrounds: rich, poor, middle class, sons of dropouts, daughters of doctors. The common bond was drugs. I got invited to parties and gatherings as long as I brought my share. I was fitting in someplace. I had become an addict.

To the Point:

Drugs provide a high for the user to ward off reality. Why give that up when it feels so good? Dosage must increase with extended use to provide the same high. Eventually, other drugs are used to find new and more fantastic highs.

When Drugs *Become* the Problem

Most experts will not only disagree with what I have to say in this section but might likely stand in fiery protest. However, I firmly believe in each statement.

Drug abuse is NOT a disease. A disease is not something a person chooses to get. Certainly, there is evidence of genetic ties in some addicts which make them more prone to becoming an addict but despite that, drug use is a choice. Granted, it is a choice that eventually eliminates the user's ability to continue to choose. Drugs do take over. That does not make it a disease. Treating drug abuse as a disease by anyone trying to help is a mistake. Once you allow the user to identify the drug as the problem, they easily avoid confronting the true reasons why they began using. Disease philosophy gives the user a convenient out, an easy way to explain his abuse. It enables users to avoid any responsibility for using a substance and allows them to hide from the reasons they became addicts.

Drugs (initially) are not the problem. Drugs are the solution many kids seek. Drug abuse is a symptom of a pending disaster, but the real illness is what creates the abuse. Kids abuse drugs to escape, self-medicate, avoid pain, and find acceptance, not because of peer pressure. Allowing peer pressure as an excuse lets the abuser avoid the real problems. Teens and adults use drugs to numb emotional pain. The drug does not cause that initial pain.

Let's try an example to explain this one: Kids on drugs are suffering –however, they were suffering before they began using drugs. When you suffer from an ailment, you take something for it. If I have a terrible sinus infection with a runny nose and it keeps me from doing my job of teaching, I take a decongestant to correct that problem. The decongestant temporarily cures my runny nose but it also makes me drowsy. I can teach, but I am not as effective as I could be. The principal walks into my classroom to observe our progress and notices my sleepy and lethargic nature. His immediate observation leads him to the conclusion that I am sleepy and thus not performing up to standards. He suggests I get more sleep at night, or that I stop taking the decongestant, neither of which will help my runny nose. Using this analogy to explain how society looks at drug abuse, the ailment that needs to be treated is perceived to be the drowsiness, not the runny nose. Society often sees drug abuse as the primary problem rather than what it truly is—the terrible side effect of self-medicating the real problem. The misguided efforts to stop drug abuse are thus doomed to fail.

Drugs eventually take over the user's life. Drugs do not begin the destruction of a person: they aid the destruction and eventually take over the task. That "take-over" is what most of society sees as the singular problem. Society tends to either gloss over or completely ignore the serious problems that led to the addiction. Drug addiction is an evil in and of itself. If you strip away all the reasons why someone began using and look at the result of the abuse itself, it becomes obvious why society considers drugs as THE problem. They are a problem—a big problem. But they are not THE problem.

The Three Stages of Abuse

I believe there are three stages every addict walks through in becoming addicted to drugs. It is the last stage (Stage Three) that society sees glaring at them because it is the most obvious. It is this stage with which all drug use is often incorrectly identified. It is Stage Three where the "takeover" begins, but two other important stages must precede it.

Stage One is where curiosity and disillusionment lead to experimentation. The experience is new and exciting, awesome and empowering, and perhaps a bit scary. Stage One users are just experimenting with drugs, using once a month or maybe once a week. This sporadic use can last for weeks or months but does not amount to addiction. This experimentation phase allows the user to get comfortable with the new illusions of confidence, power, mental strength and happiness—sensations that occur as long as the drug is used in moderation. The catch is that most users cannot use drugs in moderation for long.

Stage Two begins once the user is hooked and lasts anywhere from a few months to a year. Experimentation turns to experience when entering Stage Two as the user has become comfortable with the idea of getting high. This stage is characterized by frequent use, either on a weekly or daily basis and often leads to experimentation with other drugs. This is where true abuse begins as the user realizes that more frequent use equals feeling good more often. Once abuse sets in, the drug stops providing the "great feelings," and becomes less effective in hiding the bad feelings, thus requiring even heavier, more frequent use in order to recapture those great feelings. By this time the substance of choice is taking over the user's life. Moderation no longer provides the "high" they once felt, so they move forward to revitalize the drug's effect. There is no motivation to stop because stopping the abuse will bring back the pain they are trying to hide from tenfold. Remember the old adage: "If you get knocked off the horse, get right back on." You could say that the horse knocked them off and they never got back on. It's hard to face fears if you've not faced them for a while. It's similar to taking a vacation from work then realizing you have to go back. If you hate your job, that pending return is dreaded and often avoided with an additional sick day. The drug user doesn't want to go back to work on the job of coping any more than the vacationing laborer wants to go back to digging ditches.

Stage Three is where it all begins to crash in. Not only do drugs no longer provide the happiness, they also fail to hide the emotional pain. Instead, drugs begin to enhance that pain. In an effort to reverse this pattern, users will take heavy doses of the drug or mix it with other drugs and/or alcohol. Stage Three is where drugs turn the user inward and against himself. The user is likely getting high alone and unable to perform most tasks without the support of the drug. Tasks as simple as going to the mall or performing a chore must be aided by drug use to enhance or make the task tolerable. The day likely starts and ends with a dose of the drug with the time between filled with a combination of drugs. Stopping is not an option. The user thinks that at least he or she has something to help ease the pain. Quitting would mean facing reality, and reality by this point has become far too bleak and untouchable.

Apples and Oranges

Most teens do not try drugs. Many who do try drugs will never move out of Stage One and never become addicts. Kids who are experimenting are not drug addicts and if caught should not be treated as such. I've seen cases where a child who'd used marijuana only a few times was sent to a drug rehabilitation facility (where I was a counselor) and the child ended up in worse emotional pain than he was in before. Imagine taking medicine for an ailment you don't have. It can make you sick.

One case I remember involved a child who had been caught getting high with a friend. It was the fourth time he'd tried marijuana in six months. He was the type of kid that certainly would have gone on to Stage Two without some type of intervention. But when his parents and the rehab center treated him as a Stage Three addict, they hardened him and his resolve to continue to use. The way he was treated was unfair and he knew it. It made him bitter, and made him seek friendship from the heavier users he was in rehab with. He distanced himself further from his parents who he became convinced did not "understand," meaning they bought into the wrong reasons why drugs are a nightmare and treated him based on those myths. Treatment of a user in Stage Three shares few commonalties with approaching a kid in Stage One.

To the Point:

Drug abuse is complex and confusing to understand.

Addiction does not happen overnight nor does it begin a person's path to destruction. Drugs make life more dangerous, and by attaching to a person's daily behavior, they make it almost impossible for him or her to continue without them.

PART 2:
IS MY CHILD ABUSING DRUGS?

All this section can do is raise your awareness. It will not tell you "yes" or "no" when you ask if your child is on drugs. In discussing the general signs of teenage drug abuse I am not referring to the time periods when the teen is high. I'm referring to general lifestyle changes. I wish I could give you a checklist that could help you determine with certainty whether your teen is on drugs. You probably already know it is not nearly that easy.

I had a female friend in high school who was an "A" student, belonged to all the clubs, was a pom-pom girl, was elected to student council and homecoming court, wore all the best fashions and never looked like anything less than a princess. I knew she did drugs because she bought joints from me on a regular basis. She overdosed twice on cocaine and while on LSD had a miscarriage at a cocaine party. She hadn't known she was pregnant and became a mental wreck overnight. There is no simple description of what a kid on drugs looks like. I fit the typical description, but many of my peers who were users did not. This section can only give you clues, so if your teen displays some of the following signs it does not necessarily point to drug abuse. Please don't jump to conclusions based on this information—remember, you still have to read this entire book before acting!

General Signs of Abuse

People who abuse drugs and are afraid of being caught generally learn how to hide their abuse very well. Drug abuse among teens is harder to detect because the transformation from being clean or drug-free to being an addict is protracted and gradual and is masked by the normal changes of growing up. It doesn't happen overnight. If you compared a picture of me in seventh grade with a picture taken my sophomore year you would be shocked that anyone who knew me during that time could not tell I was on drugs. The transformation was astonishing yet subtle in its day to day progression. Adults around me probably passed off minor indications as simply "growing up" or a "phase" I was going through. I went from a typical kid to one who had long, uncombed, unkempt hair and wore the fashions of those who were generally associated with the drug culture—old tennis shoes, faded jeans, and a T-shirt with an unbuttoned flannel shirt over it. As I said, I was the cliché.

The following are possible signs of drug use but they can also indicate simple growing-up pangs or the quest for individuality in a teen. Eighth grade seems to be the ripe age for a kid to make dramatic changes in lifestyle and attitude. Even as a teacher, it was hard for me to tell if these changes were a result of drug abuse or a case of teenage expression of autonomy.

Appearance

The way your teenagers dress will never definitively say "they are on drugs" but it can be a clue. As I said, the "good" kids who did drugs were often considered the "preppie kids." They always dressed nice to keep up appearances. For those who buy into the culture part and parcel as I did, you will find a definite statement in how they dress and how they keep themselves. Compare photos of your children from year to year and analyze how they've changed. Rock T-shirts, flannels, torn-up jeans, and old sneakers all fit the cliché. Necklaces, earrings, rings, and any other item that can be worn with a pot leaf symbol on it are generally a giveaway. And again, just because your son begins wearing black lipstick, eyeliner and listens to "Death Metal," that does not mean he is on drugs.

Behavior

Teens on drugs will either sleep a lot more or a lot less while on drugs, depending on the drug. The "burnout" effect that marijuana produces creates an intense need for sleep at any time of the day. Teens on amphetamines (speed) may stay up most of the night occupying their time with some type of activity requiring motion (i.e. cleaning, pacing). Some kids have sudden changes in weight. Teen girls often use speed and cocaine as a dietary supplement because both significantly suppress appetite. Frequent use of other substances can also alter appetite and can affect a child's eating patterns. Emotional behaviors such as belligerence, hostility, apathy, moodiness, anger or other out of the ordinary behavior may become obvious. Lying also becomes ritual for a teen on drugs. Participation in sports or school activities may decline dramatically and grades might drop. Any significant change in behavior might point to a drug problem. Refer to the individual segments in Part 3 on each substance for more specific information.

Detection: General Signs

What Stage Are They In?

The above are general signs and can occur at any stage

of abuse. The lines between stages are blurry, especially when you are first finding out about your child's abuse. Here are some potential signs:

Stage One:

- sudden adoption of new friends
- more nighttime activity on the weekends
- occasional out of the ordinary behavior

Stage Two:

- more after school activity with friends
- more nighttime activity on school nights
- drop in grades
- lying
- ownership of paraphernalia (see Part 3: The Drugs)
- possession of small quantities of drugs

Stage Three:

- behavior problems at school or in the home
- severe apathy towards family activities
- habitual lying
- negative comments about mainstream society
- withdrawal from social and family interaction
- ownership of more exotic paraphernalia
- possession of large quantities of drugs
- poor hygiene
- adoption of older friends

How Can I Tell When My Child Is High?

What about the moments you suspect your child is high? Generally, a teenager who is high on drugs will go straight to his or her room upon arriving home to avoid any significant contact. There's nothing wrong with making it a point to engage your child in conversation if you suspect he or she is high.

Some telltale signs that your child is high include: slow reaction time, sluggish manners, overly talkative, overly active, difficulty in handling complex mental functions, inability to remember a list or even basic instructions, impaired motor skills, dilated pupils, red or hazy eyes, and lack of eye-contact during conversation. Some children become angry and argumentative when required to talk or answer questions. Again, this is generalized information. Specific signs are noted in the segments on each substance in "Part 3: The Drugs."

PART 3: THE DRUGS

My main motive in writing this book was to arm parents and concerned adults with the truth about drugs and drug abuse. As part of that aim I have included a section that briefly details many of the more popular drugs of choice among teens. These details are only a snapshot look and should not be seen as an all-inclusive study of any substance. I present the more widely used drugs first and give less attention to those that I've had limited experience with. I try to practice my own philosophy and thus don't want to speak as an expert on substances I've had no experience using, with the few exceptions being some of the more currently common drugs.

I attempt to look at each substance in the same manner, beginning with my experience with the substance. I then answer some common questions: What is it? What does it look like? How does it work? How is it used? In most cases I then address issues of cost and potential paraphernalia used in conjunction with the substance. Next I detail what the substance does to the user, usually from a first-hand perspective (meaning my experience) while adding some jargon and explanation. I finish with the potential long-term damage the substance can cause and a word on the drug's addictive properties. In some cases I give some practical advice on recognizing the signs of use of this substance in a teen.

The following drugs are detailed in this section: marijuana, alcohol, amphetamines (speed,) methamphetamine, cocaine, inhalants, Ritalin, ecstasy, heroin, and LSD. Information on other substances may be obtained from resources listed at the end of this book.

Marijuana

My Experience

My experience with this drug has been the centerpiece in explaining my perspective on drug abuse among teens and need not be repeated, so, let's get to the more technical discussion of this substance.

What Is It?

Marijuana (also known as "pot" or "dope") is the product of the hemp plant. Professional growers, who have elaborate systems to keep their crops healthy and hidden, often grow it in basements and attics. Due to this ingenuity, most marijuana bought in this country is grown in the United States. Much of the marijuana I bought and used came from such sources—not from Mexico or other foreign countries where many people falsely assume this drug is grown. Marijuana is estimated to be second only to corn as the largest cash crop in the United States. Growers can buy seeds on the Internet from foreign suppliers (whether it's legal in that country or not) or order them out of a catalog (seed banks) from legal foreign growers. There are dozens of types of marijuana just as there are dozens of types of tomato or lettuce plants. Some types of marijuana have been crossbred with others to create "superpotent" plants. After the plant has matured, it is harvested and dried. The leaves produce "buds" which are the primary source of the product, appearing in the shape of a small compact cocoon of green and brown. Once dried, the plant is ready for use. In its smokable form it has many different appearances. Some marijuana looks like the seasoning thyme or oregano in its ground form. Other types have red, bright green, or even yellow fibers or hairs in them.

How Does It Work?

The psychoactive (mind-altering) chemical in marijuana is called delta-9-tetrahydrocannabinol, or THC, one of over 300 chemicals in a marijuana plant. The strength of the drug depends on the amount of THC it contains. In the 1960's, most marijuana had a low THC content of 1 to 3 percent. Today, potencies are said to average 15 to 25 percent depending on the variety and the form it takes. By-products such as hashish (better known as hash, a sticky resin obtained from a female plant's flowers) and hash oil (a tar-like liquid distilled from hashish) are very potent forms of the drug.

Trends in Adolescents' Annual Use of Marijuana

% Who Used in Past Year

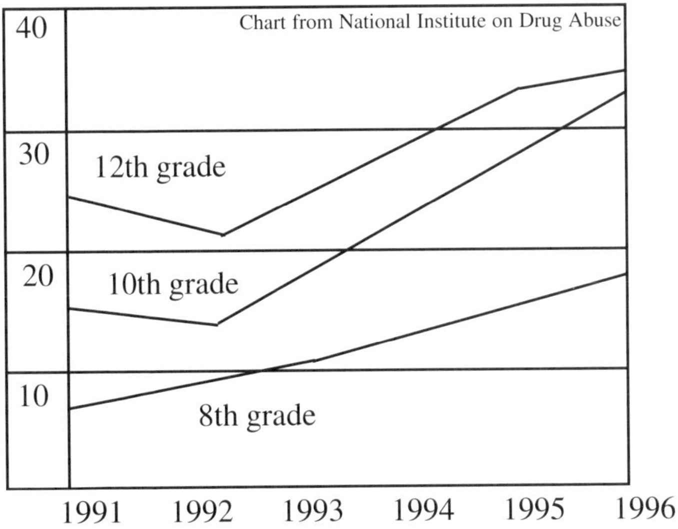

How Is It Used?

The most common method of using marijuana is smoking it. There are a variety of items used to smoke marijuana, which are listed on the next page under "paraphernalia." Marijuana can also be eaten to produce a "high" but this method is expensive because more is needed to create the desired effect.

Cost and Availability

Marijuana is sold in a variety of quantities at a variety of prices. The most common size purchase is an eighth or a quarter of an ounce. Usually the product is packaged in a clear plastic sandwich bag. Cost of an eighth of marijuana can vary from $15 to $40 depending on the potency of the pot. An eighth ounce of pot can be rolled into four to eight joints which equals about sixteen to thirty-two doses depending on potency. Possession of larger amounts such as ounces or even quarter pounds tends to indicate intent to "deal" or sell the drug. Ownership of a weight scale strongly indicates the same.

Paraphernalia

The term "paraphernalia" refers to the devices used to smoke marijuana or use any other illegal substance. Some marijuana paraphernalia include:

- **a pipe** - works in the same manner as a tobacco pipe but most pipes used for marijuana were made for pot-smoking and come in all shapes, sizes, and colors.
- **one-hitter** - a three-inch-long, pen-sized round, straight metal pipe, which can be packed with one "hit" of marijuana.
- **dugout** - some one-hitters are contained in a narrow rectangular wooden box called a "dug-out." One narrow hole at the top of the box is

for the pipe and a larger hole is for holding up to an eighth ounce of marijuana. Ironically, the dugout was invented in my hometown by a local record store owner.

- **joint** - loose marijuana rolled into a cigarette using rolling papers (easily obtained from gas stations).
- **bong** - a plastic tube of varying lengths and widths with a pipe bowl sticking out at an angle towards the bottom. The smoker inhales through the open end of the tube while lighting the bowl full of marijuana. Sometimes water is placed at the bottom of the tube creating a "water-bong," which cools the smoke as it travels through the tube.
- **sneak-a-toke** - a metal tube that looks like a large bullet, tapered at both ends. One end contains the marijuana, which is covered by a screw-in cap used to reduce the amount of burning smoke.
- **blunt** - a sliced-open cigar in which tobacco is replaced by marijuana.

Other Paraphernalia

- rolling papers
- cigarette lighters
- camera film cases - in which marijuana can be kept
- roach clip - an electrical clip used to smoke the last portion of a joint (which is called a roach)
- hemostat - made for surgeons, these are used like a roach clip
- pot leaf symbols on anything
- small weight scale
- eye drops - to clear red eyes after smoking

FACT BOX: Slang Terms
Slang terms for marijuana include dope, pot, herb, grass, weed, Mary Jane, reefer, blunt, dirtweed, brown dope, skunk, chronic, sense, or ganja.

What Does It Do To The User?

While High

Within minutes of smoking marijuana, the user will experience a euphoric feeling and a sense of displacement. It is a feeling that cannot properly be explained. Oddly, the initial feelings of alter-reality are similar to the heady feel of the onset of the flu. The high empowers, gives confidence, enhances every sense, and makes everything funny. The initial high lasts for 30 to 90 minutes but usually begins to taper off within 30 minutes. Marijuana reduces coordination; slows reflexes; interferes with the ability to measure time, distance, and depth; derails concentration; creates a dry mouth (known as cotton mouth); makes eyes bloodshot; and increases heart rate. After the apex of the high is reached the user will experience hunger (referred to as "the munchies") and eventually severe fatigue (called "burn-out" by users).

QUICK TIPS
DETECTION:
The Signs of a Kid who is High on Marijuana

These signs are not all inclusive, nor do they definitively point to drug abuse

- long or weary looking face
- seems dizzy and has trouble walking
- problems with speech
- delayed and impaired critical thinking
- silly and giggly behavior for no reason
- red, bloodshot, squinty eyes
- has a hard time remembering things that just happened
- avoids direct eye contact or conversation
- goes straight to his/her room

Effects of Chronic Use

Users who smoke on a daily or even weekly basis do not experience the same extreme euphoria they did when first smoking pot. Generally, they feel all the previously mentioned effects except the humor and the feeling of empowerment. It is this loss of once-felt extreme euphoria that leads users to seek different, more potent drugs to recapture that feeling. Chronic fatigue is always present whether high or not. Sometimes depression accompanies chronic use. Frequent colds and minor respiratory problems are also present. Loss of motivation, ambition, and a development of apathy towards nearly everything may become evident.

Known Long-Term Effects of Marijuana Use

Long-term memory is damaged, reasoning is slowed (but can be regained), nerve cells are destroyed, the immune system can be permanently damaged, and the respiratory system may be affected. I do not know of one documented case of death due to overdose, but, as with alcohol, it impairs a driver's ability to properly operate a car. This segment is titled "Known" long-term effects because we simply do not know what all the long-term effects are. There are over 300 chemicals in marijuana and researchers have yet to identify their functions.

Addiction

There are no scientific studies to support the notion that marijuana is physically addictive. Its strong grasp is mostly psychological.

Testing Your Teen

If you suspect your kid is high on marijuana there are some simple things you can do to test him or her without revealing that you are suspicious. These tests can also be used to detect the use of other drugs.

IMPORTANT NOTE:
Don't try these until you've finished this book.

Trap in conversation. If your child comes home from school late after hanging out with friends and habitually avoids conversation or goes straight to his or her room, start a conversation. Knock on the door and simply initiate a "How's the weather?" type of discussion. Listen and look for broken sentences, word mistakes, lack of eye contact, and nervous speech.

Perform tasks. Give your child tasks to perform that require several directions. Watch for simple mistakes of memory or awkward confused movement.

Do math. Ask for help with some mathematical equations, such as seeing if you were cheated on a grocery bill, and look for the same behavior mentioned earlier.

Use their paranoia against them. Kids who are high are kids who are very paranoid about getting caught. In addition, the drug itself creates paranoia. No matter how normal they may be acting, they are constantly questioning whether those around them (parents, teachers, other teens) know if they're high. Ask them specific questions about what they've been doing, where they were, whom they were with. Do they get overly defensive?

Proximity games. This is my favorite in detecting use among my high schoolers. A person who is high does not react well to motion. Use broad sweeping hand gestures (side to side, near and far) and animated facial features when talking to them (of course, these must be within reason, acting like a clown will tip your hand!) This movement tends to create confusion in their movements and makes them question their ability to hide their high, quite possibly bringing a look of fear on their face meaning "Do they know!?!"

IMPORTANT:

I do not necessarily recommend using these "tricks" as they can backfire if you aren't casual enough when using them. If you choose to try them, it is imperative that you finish this book first. It is also imperative that you **not** immediately confront your child if you suspect your child is high. We'll address "confrontation" in the next section.

FACT BOX

Facts about Marijuana

According to The National Institute on Drug Abuse (NIDA), the 1994 National Household Survey on Drug Abuse:

- Marijuana contains six times the carcinogens that cigarettes do
- Marijuana is the most used illegal drug in the U.S.
- An average of 10 million Americans use marijuana each month.

NIDA's 1995 "Monitoring the Future" study found that from 1991 to 1995, marijuana use in the 12 months before the surveys rose from:

- 23.9 to 34.7% among **12th graders**
- 16.5 to 28.7% among **10th graders**
- 6.2 to 15.8%among **8th graders**.

A U.S. Government study found:

- Over 70 million Americans over the age of 12 have tried marijuana at least once.
- 50% of teenagers try marijuana before they graduate from high school

==========================

Source: http://www.nida.nih.gov/NIDA_Notes/NNVol11N2/MarijuanaTearoff.html (public domain)

Inhalants

My Experience

I often abused inhalants in conjunction with other drugs. I remember frequently breaking into a nearby lumberyard with a friend in order to smoke marijuana in seclusion. One night he brought with him a bottle of "Rush," an illegal synthetic inhalant. He held it under my nose to the point that I could not function. Most inhalants can make the user black out and can cause temporary paralysis or a numbing of the body. I honestly can't remember why these were such desirable effects. The more I sniffed, the longer it took to black out. It's similar to the feeling of getting up too fast after a nap or, if you've had the misfortune of going into shock, it feels similar to its onset. I've known a few individuals in my life who have abused inhalants, such as model airplane glue, to the point of causing noticeable, irreversible brain damage. I know of one boy who died from heart failure as a result of his abuse of inhalants.

As a teacher I've had the misfortune of discovering a multitude of eighth graders abusing inhalants in the form of thick permanent markers and white correction fluid. These forms of inhalants are easy to hide and easy for a teacher or parent to write off as basic school supplies.

What Is It?

An inhalant is any substance that gives off fumes or gases which when inhaled cause a mind-altering effect. The practice of using inhalants is often referred to as "huffing." The list of inhalants available to users is extensive and includes model airplane glue, nail polish, household solvents, markers (very popular among young teens), helium from a balloon (which adults see as harmless because of its noticeable effects on a person's speech, creating the Mickey Mouse effect), nitrous oxide (sometimes called "whippets"), even gasoline, and a variety of synthetic substances. Nitrous oxide, a gas used as a painkiller in dentistry, is a very popular form of inhalant and is readily available to children in a variety of forms. Sadly, toy stores that sell pellet guns or racing cars that require small silver tubes of compressed nitrous oxide as a propellant are common outlets for nitrous oxide purchase.

How Does It Work?

Inhalants act on the body's central nervous system by slowing down respiratory and circulatory functions. They often restrict blood flow to the brain.

How Is It Used?

The user inhales the substance through the nose or mouth.

Cost and Availability

The cost of inhalants is practically free. They can be obtained in the home, at stores, or on the streets.

Paraphernalia:

- any container with a chemical smell (pill bottles, jars)
- rags - used to absorb an inhalant to prepare it for use
- plastic or paper bags - used to hold an inhalant. The user then breathes into the bag.
- round, 3-inch-long silver tubes (containing nitrous)

What Does It Do To The User?

While High

The effects of using an inhalant last for no longer than 30 to 60 seconds. The user initially feels an intense "head-rush" (a feeling of blacking out or lightheadedness) due to the lack of oxygen allowed to the brain. This can also cause temporary paralysis, blindness, and a general numbing of all senses. Often a sense of well being or the feeling of being temporarily separated from reality (delirious) accompanies and follows the "rush."

QUICK TIPS:
DETECTION

The Signs of a Kid who has Recently Abused Inhalants

- breath and or hands have a chemical odor
- slurred speech
- poor balance/coordination
- a glazed look in the eyes
- rash or redness around the lips

Effects of Chronic Use

Chronic use can produce nosebleeds, headaches, and eye pain, a chronic tired feeling, sores on the mouth and nose, irritability, muscle and joint pain, and distinct changes in personality.

Potential Long-term Effects

Less research has been done on the long-term effects of inhalants. Regardless, it is widely accepted that long-term abuse can damage kidneys, liver, the nervous system, and the brain. Inhalant abuse can kill by causing respiratory or heart failure.

Addiction

Inhalants can be both physically and psychologically addictive depending on the substance.

FACT BOX
Facts about Inhalants

- Unlike use of other drugs, which continues to increase through 12th grade, inhalant use peaks in 8th or 9th grade.
- In 1996, 8.0% of Indiana 8th graders reported using inhalants on a monthly or more frequent basis.
- In 1996, 18.3% of Indiana 9th graders reported using inhalants at least once in their lifetimes.

Source: *http://www.drugs.indiana.edu/publications/iprc/factline/inhal.html*

Amphetamines (Speed)

My Experience

I started taking speed to counteract the side effects of marijuana. I was always tired and sleepy, (more commonly referred to as being "burned out") giving the impression of laziness. The most horrible incident I experienced occurred while trying to maintain my ability to play sports. The more I became immersed in the use of marijuana, the more I suffered from severe fatigue. I was the goalie of our high school soccer team and at one time was considered to be pretty good. I took speed before one game to counteract some severe fatigue that made me sluggish and slow. Instead of waking me up, the drug caused dizziness, nausea, and a horrible lightheaded feeling. Needless to say, the opposing team scored several goals before I was removed late in the first half. Regardless of that outcome, I continued to take speed before hockey games. After coming off the ice during a game my heart would race to the point I thought it would explode. Why did I continue? I was a drug addict.

What Is It?

Amphetamines are most commonly referred to as "speed." They are stimulants that usually come in capsule or tablet form in a variety of shapes and colors. Amphetamines are sold legally by prescription for obesity and narcolepsy (a sleeping disorder). These drugs are also readily available through advertisements in "less than mainstream" magazines and come in dozens of varieties. Amphetamines are popular among teenage girls due to the drug's appetite suppressing qualities.

How Does It Work?

Amphetamines increase activity in the central nervous

system and have an effect that is similar to that of the body's own adrenaline. Amphetamines are similar to cocaine and methamphetamine in that they give the user increased energy and heightened concentration. They are less potent than cocaine and methamphetamine but dangerous nonetheless.

> **FACT BOX: Slang Terms**
> Slang terms for amphetamines include speed, uppers, white crosses, hearts, go, zip, or fuel.

How Is It Used?

The most common method of using speed is by taking it orally. Pills or capsules are the most common form.

Cost and Availability

Cost varies but amphetamines are generally inexpensive (less than a dollar per pill) and available from a variety of legal and illegal sources.

What Does It Do To The User?

While High

Amphetamines create heightened energy, a sense of well being, feelings of intense concentration and perceived accuracy in the performance of tasks. A typical dose can last from 3 to 6 hours.

Signs of and Effects of Chronic Use

Chronic use can create a host of problems including

dramatic and prolonged changes in sleeping and eating habits or sleeplessness for days, severe weight lose, irreversible damage to blood vessels in the brain, and sores on the body.

QUICK TIPS:
DETECTION

The Signs of a Kid who is High on Amphetamines

- over-activity
- exaggerated body movements
- flush look—redness on the face, arms, or chest
- dramatic mood swings
- fast and excited speech
- decreased attention span
- restlessness
- anxiety
- repetitive behavior patterns

Addiction

The potential for physical addition is high. Tolerance for the drug builds quickly in the user's system requiring higher doses of the drug to an incredible point of up to twenty times the initial dose to attain the same high. Withdrawal symptoms are dominated by severe and disabling fatigue.

Methamphetamines

My Experience

This drug was not yet as popular and available as it is today during my passage through the drug culture. As a result, I have never tried methamphetamines. I place them next on the list because of their similarity to amphetamines. I spend time every summer with friends on an Indian reservation in the Northwest where abuse of this drug is widespread; some of my information comes from that source. The damage it has done to families and their culture is enormous.

What Is It?

Methamphetamine is a white, bitter-tasting crystal powder (from what I've been told) that has grown in popularity since the late 80's. It is most commonly referred to as "meth," or "crank." Pure methamphetamine hydrochloride is the smokable form of this drug (referred to as "crystal meth") and is far more potent and deadly.

How Does It Work?

Methamphetamine is a stimulant that affects the central nervous system. It provides the user with increased energy and heightened concentration. Traditionally individuals trying to fight fatigue or lose weight used the drug. Methamphetamine is closely related to amphetamines as it produces a similar but more potent effect. The difference is that meth creates a high similar to that of cocaine whereas amphetamines produce the effect of several cups (or pots) of coffee. Extended use of meth can produce sleeplessness for days.

How Is It Used?

Methamphetamine can be sniffed through the nose, injected, or smoked. Items used to smoke crystal meth include a variety of small pipes or it can be rolled into a cigarette or a marijuana joint. Paraphernalia used for sniffing meth are similar to those listed in the section on cocaine.

What Does It Do To The User?

While High

Snorting meth produces euphoria similar to cocaine's effect. Its initial effect, which occurs within seconds of use, is an immediate and intense heightened feeling. Smoking meth greatly enhances the high. While on the drug the user can feel energetic, may have increased physical activity, increased heart rate, decreased appetite, and may become irritable, confused, anxious or even aggressive—or so I've been told. In some cases, hypothermia, convulsions, chest pain and even heart failure are possible with first time use—this I've seen.

Effects of Chronic Use

Methamphetamine can cause irreversible damage to blood vessels in the brain which can result in the user suffering a stroke. Extended abuse can also result in prolonged paranoia, hallucinations, repetitive behavior patterns, and delusions.

Addiction

This drug is highly addictive from a psychological standpoint.

Detection

The signs of a person who is high on methamphetamine are similar to those occurring in amphetamine use.

Cocaine

My Experience

Cocaine is a ruthless substance. It gives the user fantastic feelings of contentment and confidence. For me, coming down from the high was horrible. It gave me the sensation of being on a train that was coming to a screeching halt. My fears and self-doubt returned just as quickly and if I wanted the feeling back, I had to do more. The operative word there is *had*. I felt as though I *had* to have that feeling. The more I *had* to have that feeling, the more it took to produce that feeling. Nosebleeds became common annoyances but that didn't matter. I got so desperate for that feeling that I'd continue to sniff cocaine during a nosebleed. I finally reached a point as a senior in high school when I overdosed using a combination of alcohol, marijuana, and cocaine—mostly cocaine. I went blind for ten minutes then deaf, finally passing out and vomiting on the floor. I woke in a cold and clammy sweat to see my friends hovering over me. All they could think of was what they could do for me instead of calling an ambulance. An ambulance would bring police and questions they'd prefer not to answer. What was worse was that I shared their fear. They laid me on a couch. That's the last I remembered until morning. Two days later I was using cocaine again.

Cocaine is the one substance that still scares me today in regards to my own abusive tendencies. The only reason I got out of the abuse (at the age of 20) was because my supplier got arrested and I couldn't find any for months. By then I had put my abuse into perspective and realized how deadly this drug was to me, and I simply stopped looking. During college, though, whenever the opportunity arose, I took it.

What Is It?

Cocaine is a powerful stimulant made from the leaves of the coca bush, which is found in South America. It is part of a family of drugs known as alkaloids, which also includes caffeine and nicotine. The coca leaves are turned into a paste, and then heated with hydrochloric acid to produce the most common form of the drug: a white, compacted crystal-like substance similar in appearance to hardened sugar or flour. After production, the purest form of the cocaine changes hands several times through a variety of distributors until it reaches the user. Each distributor "cuts" or adds other substances to the cocaine to increase its volume, thus bringing more dollar profit. Cocaine is often cut with flour, amphetamines, talc, or other substances such as powdered vitamins. I'd cut my own with crushed, chewable Vitamin C tablets to make it last longer. I've heard of some instances where rat poison has been used to cut cocaine. By the time it reaches the abuser the potency has been reduced by a variety of "garbage" substances.

Crack

Crack is the cheap smokable form of cocaine that has been processed with ammonia or baking soda and water into hardened chunks, or rocks. When smoked, this substance reaches the brain more quickly than snorting the powdered form, thus bringing a more intense and immediate high. Crack, as well as heroin, is readily accessible in urban settings but can also be found in suburban and rural areas.

How Does It Work?

Cocaine works by increasing the activity of neurotransmitters in the brain creating an effect similar to amphetamines (speed).

How Is It Used?

The most common method of using cocaine is sniffing the substance into the nose where it enters the blood stream through nasal tissue. Cocaine is placed on a mirror or other smooth, hard surface to prepare it for use. A razor blade is used to mince the substance into a fine powder making it easier to inhale. Using the razor blade, the user them forms the powder into short lines, about two inches long and an eighth inch wide. Obviously, heavier users make larger "lines." The user then takes a short tube or straw and sniffs the powder into the nose. Some users will also take samples on the tip of their fingers or touch it to the tongue or gums to feel the numbing effect of the drug. Other methods include smoking and injection.

Cost and Availability

Cocaine is an expensive drug ranging from $100 to $300 a gram. The average intake of a moderate user is a quarter to a half gram per use with daily usage varying. Cocaine is not as readily available as marijuana or speed but can be obtained on the street or through go-betweens in school or in the neighborhood. Due to its cost, cocaine tends to be purchased for "special occasions" or weekends rather than used daily by Stage Two abusers. Stage Three abusers of cocaine will do almost anything to obtain the money to support their habits.

Paraphernalia

Some common items users employ to sniff cocaine:

- cut straws used for snorting
- tubes - 3 inches long, one quarter inch round. Sometimes tightly rolled dollar bills are used as tubes for snorting.
- razor blades

- small mirror - used to make “lines”
- small spoon - known as a coke spoon, also used for sniffing the substance.
- coke bullet - object shaped like a large bullet with a hole at the top and a small chamber in the center which contains cocaine. Through use of a tiny knob, the user can “load” one snort into the top of the bullet.

What Does It Do To The User?

While High

After snorting cocaine the user feels a surge of energy (often referred to as being “wired”), heightened confidence, pleasure, and a sense of power. Heart rate and blood pressure also increase dramatically. These effects only last for 20 to 30 minutes. The effects of coming off a high can include fatigue and depression.

Effects of Chronic Use

Heavy use of cocaine can produce nosebleeds, insomnia, paranoia, aggression, and depression. Overdosing on cocaine can lead to heart failure. The deadly reputation of crack cocaine is due to its more potent ability to stop a human heart cold.

Addiction

Cocaine is extremely addictive—both physically and psychologically. Cocaine can take over the life of the user. I had a high school friend who sold every thing he owned and a few things he didn’t to support his habit.

FACT BOX
Facts about Cocaine

The Partnership for a Drug-Free America reports:

Studies in monkeys have shown that animals will work very hard (press a bar over 10,000 times) for a single injection of cocaine, choose cocaine over food and water, and take cocaine even when this behavior is punished. People addicted to cocaine behave similarly.

More Facts

- Data shows that cocaine use among high school seniors has been on a downward trend since its peak in 1985.
- The proportion of seniors who have used cocaine at least once in their lifetimes dropped from 17.3% in 1985 to 7.1% in 1996.
- In 1996, 6.5% of 10th graders had tried cocaine at least once, up from 5.0%in 1995.
- The percentage of 8th graders who had ever tried cocaine rose significantly from 2.3% in 1991 to 4.5%in 1996.

========================

source: http://www.nida.nih.gov/NIDACapsules/NCCocaine.html (public domain)

Alcohol

My Experience

Alcohol frequently accompanied my illegal drug abuse. I had numerous terrifying experiences in abusing this substance, often binge drinking to the point of unconsciousness. I was lucky (legally speaking) that the drinking and driving awareness campaign was in its infancy when I was a heavy drinker otherwise I would surely have a criminal record having been caught several times by the police for possessing alcohol in a parked vehicle.

Due to the unique and complex nature of its use and abuse by teens I feel to properly approach this substance would require a separate manuscript. I only briefly detail this venom here to remind you of its hold on our nation. It is the single most abused drug by teens and is responsible for more teen deaths than all other substances combined. The rules for abusing illegal drugs apply to alcohol with a few exceptions. For instance, I do believe that peer pressure and social pressure can play a large role in the use of alcohol (where peer pressure is overstated in the use of other drugs) since it is legal and is a widely accepted drug of choice among teens and adults.

Without great detail, I would simply say that alcohol, though legal, is as (if not more) emotionally and physically dangerous, destructive and deadly as any illegal drug. Do not treat abuse or even use of this drug as a phase your kid is going through. Parents tend to tacitly condone a teenager's use of alcohol as long as he or she "doesn't drink and drive" which is a sad trade-off. In some cases adults laugh off a teenager's first hangover and let the matter go. The danger is that it is probably the easiest type of drug abuse to ignore.

FACT BOX
Facts about Alcohol:

- Alcohol is the leading cause of drug-related deaths among teens.
- More than 6,000 teenagers died in alcohol-related traffic accidents in 1995.
- Alcohol is the most commonly used drug in the United States.
- Alcohol is the easiest and cheapest drug for a teenager to obtain.

=======================

Source: *A Parent's Guide To Prevention, U.S. Department of Education*

LSD

My Experience

I certainly don't enjoy sharing these stories with the world. In many cases I haven't thought of these experiences for many years and probably would have preferred they remain lost. I share them to help you get a glimpse into what these drugs do, though you can never truly understand any experience until you've been in those shoes. A common mistake made by intervening parents is claiming to know what drugs do when in fact their knowledge is from second- or more often third-hand stories. I mention my distaste for sharing these stories now because LSD is the drug that created the single worst memory from my years of abusing drugs, a memory I reluctantly share later in this section.

What Is It?

LSD (lysergic acid diethylamide), most often referred to as "acid," is a hallucinogen discovered in 1938 and one of the more powerful illegal drugs on the market. It is created from lysergic acid, which is found in a fungus that grows on rye and other grains. The United States Government allegedly used this substance as a test substance on military personnel in the late 1950's for the purpose of mind control. It failed. How the substance found its way into the general population is a matter of speculation. How it found its way to me is obvious: I was a drug addict willing to try any substance that promised a new sensation.

LSD comes in the form of tablets, capsules, small squares of paper, and occasionally liquid form. Often LSD is placed on "blotter paper," (sheets of absorbent paper), and then divided into small squares (often decorated), with each square (anywhere from one-half inch to an inch square) representing one dose.

How Is It Used?

LSD is taken orally. Blotter paper is placed in the mouth and held there until the paper disintegrates. Gelatin and liquid can be put in the eyes.

Cost and Availability

This drug is everywhere and is inexpensive, costing anywhere from $1 to $20 a dose.

> **FACT BOX: Slang Terms**
> Slang terms for LSD include acid, doses, hits, microdot, trips, drops.

What Does It Do To The User?

While High

A trip begins 30 to 60 minutes after the user takes a dose of the drug and lasts for up to 12 hours. The physical effects of LSD are far less obvious than other drugs but include dilated pupils, higher body temperature, increased heart rate and blood pressure, sweating, loss of appetite, sleeplessness, dry mouth, and possible tremors. The best way to describe what psychedelic substances such as LSD do to a user's mind is that it warps time, space, reality and self-perception. The common objects we encounter in our daily lives suddenly seem odd and out of place and become fixtures to be studied and understood in a different context. Nothing is unchallengeable. During one "trip" I remember staring at the label of a can of bug spray for what seemed to be hours. In reality, it was likely that I looked at the object for a minute or two. The bug spray can was certainly nothing to be marveled at except for the fact that the pictured plants on the label were growing before my eyes and the cartoon bug on the lid was humming a song.

Indeed, the profound lure of psychedelics is their unique characteristic of creating hallucinations, illusions and optical tricks that seem very real: walls move, music can be "seen," faces can change shape and color. Imagine how bizarre, funny, and scary normal objects and experiences are on LSD, and then picture the potential of not so ordinary experiences. Which brings me to my story. Without too much drama I'll get to the point. A friend who sat next to me in a high school typing class died tragically on prom night. She and her 16-year-old boyfriend, armed with a day-old license and a new Camero, were thrown from the car as they raced down the street. Yes, alcohol was involved. Worse, the wreck occurred in the front yard of another friend of mine who didn't spare any bloody detail in telling me about what he saw. His description of the twisted wreck and the unrecognizable condition of the young teens was haunting. I went to the open-casket wake carrying those images in my mind while tripping on LSD. The wake was bad enough to leave everyone present with scarring memories... the funeral home had reconstructed her face for the event when they should have simply closed the casket. It was a horrible sight compounded by the effects of LSD.

I share this because it makes sense to me now. How would I cope with such loss? How would I handle my first wake, my first funeral: by taking the most powerful drug I could get and letting it cope for me. Instead of helping me cope, it turned an already nightmarish scene into an unbearable event. Besides the visual horrors, I was hearing a dozen different voices saying a dozen different things from inappropriate jokes to urgings to take unspeakable actions. With the voices was a score of different sounds and noises, bells whistles, tones—all at once; it was maddening. What I saw and heard I will not say. I will end by acknowledging the fact that I was so lost and desperate to numb all emotional pain at this point in my life and drug use that I willingly and unknowingly took steps that would lead to near psychosis.

Effects of Chronic Use

Permanent brain damage is a likely outcome of chronic use. The ability to focus on simple tasks, short-term memory, and other critical thinking skills are destroyed. I wasn't too fond of LSD because its effects weren't that appealing, so I didn't do more than five hits in my entire life. My psychedelic of choice was mushrooms which create similar effects. Frankly, LSD was a bit scary to me because it was impossible to detect if it had been tampered with or was even the right substance. Others didn't have the caution I had and paid for it with the loss of their ability to ever think clearly again. An older kid we'd often see wandering the neighborhood was always ripped on LSD. Occasionally he'd stop and ask for directions to places he'd been a hundred times or ask for LSD. Even when he wasn't on the drug, he seemed very lost and listless. I thought he was homeless, as did my friends, until we learned he lived in the upper westside with his wealthy family.

The wrong mixture or improperly measured dose of LSD could simply lead to a living nightmare, known as a "bad trip." I luckily never had a bad trip but I had several friends who did. The resulting behavior ranged from crippling fear and rigid catatonic states to raving madness and paranoia. While camping near the river miles outside of town, one friend got the idea that we were trying to kill him. He ran into the night shedding clothing as he went, screaming something about his clothing being poisoned. We found him the next day back home some 12 miles from the river—he had no idea how he'd gotten there.

Some LSD users experience flashbacks, or a reliving of certain aspects of the drug's effect without ever taking the drug again. A flashback can occur suddenly and without warning, months or years after the user's last trip.

Addiction

LSD is not an addictive drug. Often those who use it will decrease their use as they get older.

FACT BOX
LSD Use by Students, 1997
Monitoring the Future Study (MTF)

	8th Graders	10th Graders	12th Graders
Ever Used	4.7%	9.5%	13.6%

Ritalin

My Experience

My Ritalin use is another story I'd prefer to forget but include for your benefit. This is a drug that became popular well after my illegal drug use had stopped yet I have used and abused Ritalin. When I was a young adult in college, doctors treated my clinical depression by prescribing a variety of antidepressants, some of which left me lethargic and tired throughout the morning hours. Ritalin was prescribed to give me the jolt of energy I needed to make it to the afternoon. I don't quite understand how it works, but it calms hyperactive children and revives lethargic adults. The problem was that it worked too well, and as with many drugs, its effects began to fade as the weeks of use went on. The doctor prescribed a higher dose. Its effects began to fade again. Why ask for a higher dose when I knew I could simply take more and save a trip to the doctor. I lied about "losing the bottle" so I could get more and I abused the substance in this manner for a month. I quickly realized that I was simply repeating old habits and behaviors and resolved to stop using this drug immediately. There was the big mistake. The morning I stopped found me close to psychotic and thinking of suicide—for no apparent reason. The medication's ability to alter mood is profound and should not be taken lightly by parents considering medicating their child.

What Is It?

Ritalin, scientifically known as methylphenidate, is a medication commonly prescribed for children with attention-deficit hyperactivity disorder (ADHD) and adults with certain depressive disorders. Often, children who do not need the medication are prescribed it as a quick behavior modification fix. In my eighth grade classes, some 30 percent of my students were on Ritalin. Some children needed it to help them focus and it did just that. Most however were just kids being doped into submission by parents who didn't understand how to deal with a normal child's active behavior.

How does it Work?

Ritalin stimulates the central nervous system and works on a level similar to cocaine.

How Is It Used?

Ritalin is supposed to be taken orally but is often crushed into powder and snorted by kids abusing the drug.

Cost and Availability

The legal cost is relatively inexpensive. The street cost can be anywhere from $1 to $5 per dose.

Paraphernalia:

Same as those used for cocaine.

What Does It Do To The User?

While High

Ritalin calms hyperactive children and can help children with ADHD focus on their studies. Ritalin's side effects can include nervousness, loss of sleep, and changes in heart rate and blood pressure. It can also result in "toxic psychosis" or "psychotic episodes"—which I mentioned had happened to me.

Signs of Chronic Use

Same as sniffing cocaine and using stimulants.

Potential Long-Term Effects

Similar to amphetamines

Addiction

"...research funded by the National Institute of Mental Health has shown that people with ADHD do not get addicted to their stimulant medications at treatment dosages." I did not have ADHD. I did not always take the recommended doses... I felt very much addicted to this substance.

Ecstasy

What Is It?

MDMA, known as "Ecstasy" is a relatively new drug used in a manner similar to methamphetamines and amphetamines. I don't know much about this drug except that it is supposedly popular among young people attending all night dance parties known as "raves."

How does it work?

Some studies show that MDMA "destroys serotonin-producing neurons in the brain which play a direct role in regulating aggression, mood, sexual activity, sleep, and sensitivity to pain."

How Is It Used?

Ecstasy comes in a tablet form that is often branded with the Playboy bunny or Nike swoosh symbol.

Cost and Availability

Inexpensive and readily available.

What Does It Do To The User?

While High

Users report feeling heightened sensations to taste and touch as well as intense feelings of well being and contentment. Beyond this description I cannot comment on what this drug does to a user.

Potential Long-term Effects

Similar to those found with the use of amphetamines and cocaine.

Heroin

My Experience

I used to smoke a lot of opium when it was available, and I know the effects of morphine use from a nasty hospital stay, but other than these related drugs, I have never tried heroin.

What Is It?

Heroin is processed from morphine which is a naturally occurring substance taken from the opium poppy plant. Processed heroin is a white or brown powder or tar-like substance, which is injected or smoked

How does it work?

This drug works as a depressant on the central nervous system.

How Is It Used?

Heroin can be injected, smoked, mixed in a marijuana joint or regular cigarette, or snorted as powder.

Cost and Availability

Estimates vary though it is a relatively inexpensive drug.

What Does It Do To The User?

While High

After a dose by injection or snorting, users report experiencing an instant and intense feeling of relief and contentment with a warm flushing of the skin, a dry mouth, and heavy-feeling limbs. After the initial "rush," mental processing slows due to the depression of the central nervous system. Other effects include slowed and slurred speech, constricted pupils, and droopy eyelids.

Signs of Chronic Use

Chronic use can result in loss of weight, graying of the skin, "track" marks from repeated injections, lethargic movement and slow thought processes.

Potential Long-term Effects

Potential physical damage can be done to a chronic user such as collapsed veins, infection of the heart lining and valves, and liver disease. Heart and respiratory complications including pneumonia may result from the poor health condition of the abuser, as well as from heroin's damaging effects on respiration. Street heroin often has additives that do not dissolve and result in the clogging of blood vessels, which can cause infection or even death.

Addiction

Regular heroin users develop tolerance to the substance resulting in increased use to achieve the same effects. Heroin is highly addictive though withdrawal symptoms in heavy users can be less severe than those in alcoholics.

FACT BOX
Heroin Use by Students

Monitoring the Future Study, 1997:

	8th-Graders	10th-Graders	12th-Graders
Ever Used	2.1%	2.1%	2.1%

======================

Source: NIDA, DEA

PART 4: DEALING WITH THE PROBLEM A STARTING POINT

Once again: The information contained in this book is based on opinion and driven by experience. It is your task to make decisions regarding your child or student. Oftentimes books and pamphlets of this nature try to give parents and teachers definitive answers to a problem when the fact stands that every situation requires a different reaction. Despite my continued caution towards expert testimony, I urge you to explore other sources in your quest to understand the components of prevention, intervention and treatment.

Prevention:

A Word for Teachers

When teachers try to mimic the "just say no" rhetoric of the anti-drug movement, they come across as foolish to most teens. I also remind you that by parroting these themes you are simply adding to the problem inherent to the disillusionment that often grows within a teen. Many teens truly believe they've been lied to and that adults don't understand their unique problems. Remember, speaking with authority on a subject you really have little knowledge about will get you in trouble, just as easily as teaching an academic subject you're unprepared to teach.

So, what role can you play? The "honest adult" role gives you credibility in their eyes. Teachers often buy into the "sage" advice of veterans who say, "Never let your students know you're wrong" and "Don't smile until Christmas." Why not? Reveal your humanity to your students and they'll respect you for it. When I think I am boring a class to tears with a lesson or simply failing to convey the basic message of the topic, I stop and share with them what I think is happening. Sometimes I, too, am bored with a topic and find it hard to motivate myself; other times I might not be feeling well, or simply not teaching well, and I share those feelings with my kids.

This respect—which teachers know takes time to build—goes much further when talking to students about drugs than simply hitting them on the head with rhetoric. Whenever I broach the topic, I begin with honesty: "I know you're probably going to do what you want to do regardless of what I say, but this is what I know..." I always get to them with that opener. I don't preach; I don't tell them what to do; I simply teach them what I know. I know my two cents on drug abuse will only go so far considering I only see them one hour a day, five days a week. Keep in mind that's less than 3 percent of a child's waking moments during a week (with 30+ other classmates), and you might not be as hard on yourself for not getting through. The concept here is "every little bit helps." Just make sure it is credible help.

Parents

Having a talk with your teen will not prevent her or him from abusing drugs. That may seem obvious but to watch some anti-drug television commercials it would appear to do the trick. The process of prevention is a complex combination of actions that must include many on-

and you've likely found yourself making the same mistakes they made. Even if they were "outstanding," your kid's needs are much different in many respects than your needs were while growing up. Likely, you were raised, as was I, from an industrial age mindset and we know the tech age is a far different world. Analyze what you find in researching the subject of parenting and decide which information makes sense. I often see parents struggling to find answers until they latch on to the first idea they see on TV or read in a magazine that seems right. Trust your own ability to forge an answer that is right for you and your child. Applying a packaged, one-size-fits-all response provided by "expert" advice will often fail because it is not a specially catered answer to your child's unique and dynamic situation. Don't be afraid to be a good parent based on your own conclusions.

Talking to Your Child/Students about Drugs

There are several resources that can help get a conversation rolling with your child about drug abuse if you are looking for prepackaged help. I believe the "being yourself with your child or student" approach is best. Be honest with them. Tell them your fears and give them rational reasons why you think drugs ruin lives. Don't go on about evidence and statistics you may have seen on TV, in magazines, or even in this text. Be real with them. Don't appeal to their emotions or try to scare them. Open an avenue to dialogue, not lecture. Let them know you may not understand the problem the same way they do (or think they do) but you are willing to try. There is nothing wrong with using a pamphlet or other books to find more information or other opinions. Pamphlets available from your local hospital or other resources (listed later in this book) might be useful in getting a conversation started. The best discussion though is an on-going one. Whenever you have the chance to talk about "doing the right thing," take it. It's not just an on-going conversation about drugs; it's an on-going conversation about living life.

Raising and Teaching Teens Without The Myths

Certainly, some information should be kept from children for the protection of their innocence. Kids are forced to grow up too fast in today's society and a little protection from the boogiemen of the world (who exist—I've met them!) isn't a bad thing. But weigh what you say, think, and do about <u>any</u> topic, not just drugs,and then ask yourself whether it's true. Do you really know for a fact what marijuana does to a person? Could you explain the experience of skydiving without having ever done it? Perhaps you can imagine it, but don't state that imagined idea as fact. Don't cite information you really don't know much about. Kids are clever in detecting that and once they do, your credibility is diminished. It's OK that you don't know everything. Perhaps the starting point here should be to question your own beliefs. Are you really sure why drugs are bad? You've seen countless horror stories of what drugs do to kids, but what do you really know about that lifestyle beyond an after-school special or TV commercials? This doesn't mean you must feign ignorance and give in to what others think they know. Any child's experience and perspective is no more or less unique than your own. Sharing in discussion is more than one person doing the talking and one doing the listening. Share what you know and let them share what they know—without judgment.

Teaching The Skills of Coping

In writing this section, my computer froze and I lost two pages of work. It took over an hour to do. I had to use the skills of coping to move forward despite my anger at losing all that work. I learned those skills through years of counseling as a young adult because I had lost the opportunities to learn them as a teen. How do you deal with a setback? This is the starting point in teaching children of any age how to deal with the stress of failure. Perhaps you feel angry, tearful, calm, then patient. Maybe you tell yourself "It happened and it won't ruin my day; I can move forward." Believe me, I was in a state of shocked disbelief after realizing I'd lost so much work, then I was angry to the point of giving it up for the night. Instead, I'm using it as a positive by sharing it with you. Dwelling is a negative coping skill. I don't use that one anymore (well, most of the time) because I've learned that it brings everything to a stand still. Do you share your methods of coping with your children or students? We miss so many teachable moments and opportunities to coach our kids on how to deal with daily life. For example, when junior spills his milk, how does he feel? As a youngster I remember feeling shock then fear because I had made a mess. As a child, that was a very stressful moment—as stressful as burning dinner is for me today. How do you respond? Do you say "Oh no, not again!" in a frustrated tone or do you respond with a smile on your face and a towel in your hand and say "Hey, spilled milk is like life; if you make a mess, you have to clean it up?" It is the daily stressful events—at home, school, everywhere—of a child's life that let him or her build skills to cope with the big stuff—like paying bills with money you don't have.

Good teachers are familiar with the concepts of coaching, modeling and using teachable moments to their advantage. Where were these concepts birthed? In the parent/child relationship. **Coaching** is turning a mistake, error, or problem into a teachable moment. It's called coaching for obvious reasons. That's what coaches of sports teams do; they use the mistake to help correct the action. Minor problems to us can be major events to children. Lead them to the answer; don't give it to them. By coaching your children from the start, you are teaching them the skills to cope with the stresses that can later lead to the practice of using illegal drugs as self-medication. Teachers! Don't use these methods just through the curriculum. Use them with everything that happens in class, the school halls, wherever you are in contact with your students. Coach them toward appropriate behavior rather than scolding them into submission.

Modeling is simply practicing what you preach. Share with your child/student your emotions when dealing with a stressful situation, perhaps explaining the thought process you went through to arrive at a mental solution. For example: you just got cut off on the freeway. Anger sets in, you may say a few choice words, and then you calm down, gather yourself, and continue on. If your child is with you, make sure he or she knows how you reacted on the inside—not just on the outside. Without this information, your child only sees, or hears, your outward response and learns a poor lesson on coping with that type of situation, missing out on how you got through it on the inside. If your child wasn't with you, talk about it when you get home. Share your coping strategies with your kids. It's very similar to teaching the simple gesture of saying "Thank you." If you do it, and you teach your children when and why to say it, they will likely adopt the practice as their own. In this manner, coping becomes automatic. And if you as an adult have problems with coping, well, how can you teach something until you learn it and practice it yourself?

Maintaining Discipline

Discipline means "being mean" in the eyes of a child. I've seen far too many parents who don't want to be perceived as being mean and who eventually lose control of the decision-making process with their child. I've seen teens openly ignoring all rules posted by Mom and Dad, in some cases literally cursing their parents in front of teachers. The rules were well intended, but no consequences were in place to reinforce them. The child was in control. Many drug intervention programs talk of setting specific rules regarding drug use and other inappropriate behavior. Seldom do they talk of the establishment of consequences. I won't give you an example nor will I speak to corporal punishment but I will say that the "time-out" mentality often does not work. Adults face serious consequences for breaking the law or for not being responsible for bills, for our children, even for our pets. Letting your children move through early life without stern reaction to rule breaking does not keep you in their favor; it sets them up for failure. Be honest and fair in setting rules and let your child be involved in the rule-making process (with you at the head of the conversation). Again I must speak to the flip side here as well: Leaning on your child too hard will do nothing but belittle him or her and damage confidence.

The Contract

As a teacher I've used behavior contracts with great success either to start a school year on common ground or to give ownership of consequences to a troubled kid. In some situations I've seen family contracts work very well. A contract includes as many rules as you can think of for your child with a set course of action if those rules are broken. I've seen some very fun yet serious parent/child contracts that read like a law book complete with sub-sections and clauses. I've also seen contracts specific to one behavior. Adding incentives to the contract helps as well. (For example, if weekend curfew is adhered to for six months, it will be extended one half hour.)

There are two keys that will make a contract work: One, your child (or entire family) must *ha*ve input into the rule-and-consequence-making process. A contract is between TWO or more parties. Second—look out—you must allow your child to make rules and consequences for you! (An example might be: Mom will not embarrass me by dropping me (the child) off at the front door of the mall. If she does, she must allow an extra half hour of time at the mall or pay a fine of $5.) Make a contract official with witnesses and signatures. Review and update it as your child gets older. Contracts are useful, fun to make in many cases, and they can create a deeper bond between parent and child when both sides collaborate on the contents. They also make a great platform for rationally discussing why rules and consequences are important.

Sample Contract

Item One: Curfews

I. _Teen's name___will:

A. Come home directly from school each school day unless otherwise allowed.

Consequences: (to be determined by parents)

B. Be home by 6 P.M. on school nights and 10:30 P.M. on weekend nights providing he/she makes an honest disclosure of where he/she will be until that time.

Consequences: Curfew will be shortened one hour each weekday and two hours each weekend night for every violation.

I.B.1: If these rules are adhered to for three months without problem, curfew will be extended 1/2 hour each night.

1B.2: __Teen's name_ will telephone 1/2 hour before curfew's end to request any additional time or to explain why he/she might be late.

II. _Parents' names_ will:

A. Not wait up for _Teen's name_ one of the two weekend nights in a show of trust.

Consequences: Curfew extended to midnight for one evening.

B. Also adhere to a weekend curfew of 11 P.M. when visiting with friends.

Consequences: (to be determined by the children of the family)

Building Confidence

Adults destroy confidence in children in the subtlest ways. We often forget they are still learning about <u>everything</u> and we often put them down for acting their age. The innocent act of rolling your eyes at a simple mistake can tell a child, "That was easy; how could you have missed that?" Negative comments about their failures undermine their attempts to learn. Innocent comments made in a joking manner can do the same thing. "Don't be stupid," "Grow up," "What's wrong with you," "You quit everything you start," and a hundred other negative comments you see as harmless translate very differently to a child. We all know we must encourage children at every step of growth. We often forget. Keep in mind though that a child with true confidence is not one who necessarily thinks everything she or he does is great. Confidence is attained by encouragement, not a false propping up of esteem. Adults must help teens come to <u>their own conclusions</u> about their abilities, strengths, <u>and</u> weaknesses. Again, this is a child-rearing topic that deserves a book of its own. Research the skills of parenting as rigorously as your claim to want to be a great parent.

A Different Kind of Addict

A teen free of drugs can go through exactly the same pressures as those of a kid who uses drugs. A drug-free teen is not necessarily without addictions. Excessive eating and obsession with video games are obvious alternatives, but I've seen a far more destructive pattern evolve in some teens—that of over activity. Some teens facing these pressures slowly take on so many extracurricular activities that they have little time to rest. Such activities may make a parent proud, but questions must be asked: Why are they so involved? Are they truly happy or are they trying to prove something? Or hide from something, like the fear of failure? I taught an eighth grade girl who took part in every club, played every sport, cheered on the cheerleading team, volunteered hours at the local rest home, participated in student council, handled a dozen best friends, flashed a glowing non-stop smile, and earned straight A's. She was miserable. She was under the pressure of a mother who excelled at everything and expected the same from her child. Mom was a supportive parent. She was not overbearing nor too demanding—on the surface. Subtle messages are all it took and they all translated into "You must be perfect to be successful" and her daughter believed it. Yes, she was drug-free (as far as I knew) but she was being damaged in a different manner.

Intervention:

A Word for Teachers

Three eighth-grade boys walked into my first period class reeking of marijuana and obviously stoned to the gills. What could I do? **Option 1:** Nothing. I'd done drugs before and understood that busting them and getting them in trouble with the law would do more harm than good. **Option 2:** Confront them myself with my own brand of logic and knowledge and let them know I know, giving them the best guidance I can give. **Option 3:** Send them straight to the office to be searched and questioned by the principal. **Option 4:** Call home and delicately suggest something may be wrong with their child. What would you do? What is the right choice?

Option 1 gives them another chance but ultimately leads to future opportunities.

Option 2 brings some respect my way and gives them

another chance but might lead to future occurrences because it quietly says, "It's O.K. that you're high, today."

Option 3 might mean that they are searched, and only a lighter is found. The kids return to class as high as before with smug smiles on their faces and the law on their side—students cannot be suspended or expelled on suspicion of use in most states. This ultimately undermines my authority.

Option 4 could open a whole bag of angry cats from Mom and student.

So, what did I do? All of the above at one time or another and each left me feeling horrible about the choice. I finally learned **Option 5**, which didn't leave me feeling much better. **Option 5** is to tell the counselor and let her or him deal with it through counseling, thus absolving myself of any responsibility. It is a no-win situation in which you must do the right thing over the popular or easy thing. And the right thing might vary depending on the student in question.

My Best Suggestions to a Teacher Facing this Scenario:

- Take responsibility as an adult and do something! Never ignore your suspicions by ignoring the incident; always get others involved to help.
- Do not confront a kid who is high but contact the principal or counselor immediately after the period is over so a search may be conducted.
- Find time in the following days to talk to the teen about your suspicions without being accusatory and being empathetic and understanding.
- Communicate with the parents no matter

what—it is their right to know what you suspect.
- Get your school counselor's opinion. Hopefully you can trust his or her judgment.

Parents:

Fearing your child is on drugs is stressful. It's even more stressful when you confirm the fear. You must not let that fear stop you from starting the process of understanding and helping your kid. Would you move to push your teen out of the way of a speeding bus? Even if that bus could hit you? Although you're probably joking with yourself right now, the truth is you would do anything for your child. Drug abuse is a speeding bus that will go out of control. Acting without thinking, though, would be to push your child out of danger from being hit by one bus and into the path of another.

King Of The Castle

You own your home. You pay all the bills. Your family is <u>not</u> a democracy. You brought your children into this world whether they like that or not. Walking that tightrope between protecting your children and giving them autonomy is difficult but remember this: It is easier to search your children's rooms and then explain why you did it (out of fear and love for them) than to give them free reign of their domain. You are the parent. Your job is to teach and protect, while allowing autonomy. Don't let one dominate the other. If you suspect for a slight moment that your child is doing drugs, then don't hesitate to act, even if you are sneaky about it. Your initial fear is likely true. If it is, you've done the right thing by searching their backpacks, clothes, room and its contents. If your fear is false, you've done the right thing because you care.

Where To Look

Kids are ingenious in the ways they hide their drugs. Here are some hiding places:

At home:

- Jewelry or knickknack box
- Desk and clothing drawers
- Under the bed
- In the mattress or pillow
- Taped under or behind a desk
- Under the foot of a piece of furniture
- Under the carpet
- In a sock or shoe
- In a fake decoration (i.e. fake cans of soda that have false bottoms)
- In other rooms like the bathroom - even in the front room where the family spends time.

Basically, ANY PLACE

On their person:

- Obvious places - pockets, socks, shoes
- Not so obvious - in the pants or underwear

Physical Signs: What to Look for in the Room

Small greenish-brown seeds (marijuana seeds,) tobacco smell in clothing, old sandwich bags, (used to carry marijuana,) dust-like material in old sandwich bags or on desk tops or any surface, pills of any kind, any of the previously mentioned paraphernalia, or ANY suspicious material.

Hiding the Smell of Marijuana

Hiding the smell of marijuana is no easy task. Some products such as Ozium or incense are used to kill the smell. Most teens don't care about how their room smells so if an air freshening product, incense, or scented candle is present in their room you may want to question their motives for having it.

Confrontation: My Child's on Drugs. How Do I Deal with It?

Gather Yourself

First, don't go seeking blame. Don't race through your mind to find what could have gone wrong or how you missed the signs. Anger and a sense of failure are common reactions. Dwelling on these things damages your ability to deal with the problem. Don't blame their friends. Let's move forward before analyzing what went wrong because our primary concern now is not who's at fault, but how do you help. Keep the following in mind before confronting your child:

Never Confront a Child who is under the Influence of Drugs or Alcohol.

Why? Drugs affect different people differently. Regardless of how a teen might react when confronted while high the point to be understood here is that her or his ability to cope with the confrontation in a rational manner is compromised. No one will benefit from such confrontation.

- Calm down by taking a walk around the block or by trying to watch some television.
- Discuss the situation calmly with your spouse or other relatives.
- Don't immediately assume your child is an addict. It is possible she or he is in the early stages of abuse. It is also possible that he or she will never

develop long-term abusive behaviors. Some kids do try drugs for a while and quit. If you treat that type of user as an addict you may do more damage than good. (See "The Dangers of Prevention and Intervention")

- Don't be afraid to seek help from teachers or professionals but remember to use common sense. Oftentimes these "textbook professionals" have no real sense of what drug abuse is about and will spit out the same rhetoric that I've told you to avoid. Don't agree to every course of action they suggest.

Focus On The Task

The next thing you need to do is assume everything you've been told about substance abuse was wrong—even though this may seem like poor advice (certainly there is truth amongst the falsehoods). But that must be your starting point. The fear that anti-drug rhetoric puts in the minds of parents is partially based on misinformation and misinterpretation of information. This fear then turns parents into a raw nerve. The seriousness of these myths is that drugs are indeed extremely dangerous but not as those myths or rhetoric portrays them. Why ignore that rhetoric for now? **Fear is your worst enemy in dealing with a child suffering from substance abuse.** Fear and everything that goes with it—panic, anger, tears, anguish—all work against you because these emotions immediately put you on the heap of the misinformed mainstream (remember Part 1) in the eyes of the abuser, who is your child.

To drug-affected teens, using drugs is no big deal. They feel they've proven as much to themselves and thus proven that society was wrong. Once you show extreme emotions in dealing with the problem you have proven to your child that you are one of "them," and you've pushed your efforts backward. It's as simple as this: Kids think they know what it's all about. In their confidence, they think they know that adults (you) don't know what it's all about. When you show emotions (anger, fear) that don't seem to fit what they see as being a reasonable reaction to the problem (drugs are no big deal), you've given them proof (as they see it) that you truly don't know what it's all about, regardless of what you actually know. I realize this is much easier to write or say than do. I won't for a moment say that you shouldn't be afraid. You should be very afraid. And there is nothing wrong with telling your child that you are afraid. Nor am I telling you not to act. Simply control the situation. If not, your emotions will control you and that will cripple your primary efforts.

The Approach

I can't simplify how to approach your child about what you suspect or what you've discovered. If the child has both parents in the home or a mother and father who are divorced yet participate in the child's life, both should be present. Two on one makes your task easier but if you do have help, make certain you've both read this book and have reached an agreement on what to do.

A good first opening line is an honest statement about how much you care about them, even though they may be in such a rebellious stage that such words are intolerable for them to hear. From this point there are a thousand different ways to tell them you suspect them of drug abuse. You must decide for yourself whether you want your response to be seen as genuine concern rather than accusation. Be cautious, though. Do not try to trap your child in a lie by asking, "Are you doing drugs?" waiting for the lie, then producing evidence to the contrary as proof. This does little but humiliate. Again, be honest and open, calm and patient. Don't force the truth out of them. Wait for it to come when they're ready. Don't back down though. Stick to your evidence until they accept responsibility. Your child will initially deny the truth despite any overwhelming evidence. If you need to, take a break from the conversation to allow your child to think through what is happening. This is a stressful situation to cope with—Mom and Dad now know their secret!

The Rebuttal: Emotional Manipulation

Drugs and paraphernalia were easy to hide from my parents because they were forbidden to enter my room. I used all types of mind games to achieve that status. Still, I had some ingenious hiding places, even in areas my parents frequented—like the garage. I knew which eye drops worked best to eliminate red eyes, and could remove the marijuana smell from my coat by having a friend blow cigarette smoke on me. Yes, I smelled like cigarettes, but I didn't smell like marijuana. I never did smoke cigarettes. I did not like them and my parents knew it but it was OK with Mom and Dad if my friends did. It was OK that I hung out with a "hard around the edges" crowd because I was finally fitting in—someplace. Besides, my parents refused to take that away from me because they knew I'd revolt. An issue they tried hard to avoid.

When a kid discovers that most parents hate confrontations, that kid will use it against them. I remember that a friend of mine had been caught using drugs by his mother. She called every parent in the neighborhood (which is not an unreasonable response). My mother confronted me, in tears, asking if I'd ever done drugs. Emotions were her weakness in this issue and I knew it. I acted without thinking. I calmly reassured her, easing her fear and feeding her need to not believe. I manipulated her—a skill I had learned growing up. This ended all questioning for two years. For the next confrontation I used the opposite approach. "How could you not believe me!" I said with angry dishonesty. I showed anger and played on her fear that she was losing me. "How could you accuse me of lying? I am your child." That ended all questions. People hate confrontations. Parents hate confrontations with their kids and kids know it. Don't allow your child to manipulate your fears.

Other Easy Outs

Many kids who use drugs have rationalized their drug use. Below are some comebacks a child may try to use when he's or she's been caught. Prepare for these responses by asking yourself how you would answer them.

- You smoke and drink, so why can't I?
- I have it under control.
- Everyone I know drinks or takes some kind of drug.
- Marijuana is not bad for you.
- It's only marijuana. I don't plan on taking anything stronger.
- I'm in charge of my own body.
- It's no big deal. I can quit when I want.
- I just did it once or twice. I don't even like it.

Stopping the Abuse

This is a tough topic for me to address because it is also the most delicate in regards to what steps you will take. Do you do it yourself? If so, how? Do you seek help? How? I can only give suggestions and can only offer my opinions based on my experiences. So, how did I stop?

The Most Dangerous Aspect of Drug Abuse: Getting Out

After my overdose on cocaine I began to realize that I had a problem. I didn't realize how serious it was but it did get me thinking. I started college with the same habits I had adopted as a teen. By the way, I lucked into college. I had taken the A.C.T. twice. The first time I took it I did my best to not try—not giving "half a damn" because "I wasn't going to college" as I was told by parents, adults, peers, and myself. I scored the minimum requirement for state college. The second time I took the test I was high as a kite on marijuana. I scored a few points lower. After being contacted by the state university for meeting the basic requirements, college began to look like a good way out of my hometown and a way to get away from my parents. Our relationship by this time had been strained nearly beyond repair. We rarely spoke. I packed my bags and my drug abuse and took them to college.

My freshman year, I received the best grades of my life. For whatever reason, I was beginning to see the big picture: put forth some effort, or flip burgers for a living. I chose effort. But my effort could only go so far with my drug abuse. I was getting high every day as I had done for nearly four years, only by now I was doing it alone. Every night, I got high, alone. And that began to seem strange. I wasn't as deep into the drug culture anymore because I didn't hang out with those who could extend my abuse. I was mostly smoking pot and binge drinking and generally preferred to do it alone. I began to see that as a problem. The first summer after my freshman year I decided to make some effort at stopping my abusive behavior. I went to an N.A. meeting (Narcotics Anonymous) in my hometown. These programs help many people but are steeped in religion. At that time though, it seemed to me that religion was part of the lie society was perpetrating. As soon as the prayer took place at the end of the meeting, I was determined never to go back. And I didn't.

Three more years of college and daily drug abuse passed before I tried again. I had gone years knowing that I had no control over my abuse. The longer I stayed in college (after dropping out for a semester) the wider my eyes were opened to the possibilities before me. I simply reached a point where I said to myself "That's enough." I arrived at this place after eliminating the external influences (drug addict friends) and questioning internal influences (why was I doing this to myself?) I took out my calendar and wrote "one month and one week" on the day that was five weeks away. The time period meant nothing; it just seemed poetic. I told myself I would not do drugs for that period of time. It was something I simply decided I had to do for myself. The first week was hard. I was a mental wreck and experienced some physical withdrawal symptoms such as sleeplessness and irritability. Despite that first week, I did it. I stopped using drugs for five weeks—and then promptly started smoking pot again for several months. I took the challenge again and was successful for two months and two weeks. I got high for a week, and then stopped for a week. I became a sporadic user for the next year until I decided to stop completely.

There are two points to be made here: One, I wish it were as simple as it sounds and I wish I could give you the formula that stopped my prolonged abuse. Honestly, there isn't one. Individuals are just that—unique and complex. There is no template for stopping the abuse. I had simply had enough of the self-punishing behavior, and college was opening my eyes to the potential of the world—sounds easier than it was.

The next point brings us back to those much-needed skills of coping. Remember, I had used drugs as a means of coping for eight years. Now that the drugs were gone, I fell apart. I was 22 and reacted to setback with the confidence of a 14-year-old. On top of any current setbacks, every past trauma, disappointment, and bad experience I had failed to deal with for eight years came rushing at me, seemingly at once. I was an emotional mess, and I did not know why. I quickly dropped into a pit that I almost didn't come out of. I would binge drink on the weekends, thinking I was getting by fine "drug free." I would lock myself in my apartment for days at a time, sleeping 14 to 18 hours a day to escape the staggering depression that seemed to come from nowhere. I was a mess. I looked like a sickly 40-year-old and weighed 135 pounds (I was 6 feet tall).

I finally sought counseling at the college counseling center but my embarrassment coupled with a poor counselor ended the attempt. Within weeks I gave it another shot because I was afraid I wouldn't make it to my next birthday. Luckily, I found a great counselor who helped me deal with the pain I held inside. It took nine months of one or two sessions a week. At first, the nightmare got worse. I relived every past problem and had to deal with each, as I should have when I first experienced them. The more I was exposed to the past I had failed to cope with, the more depressed I got. I liken it to this analogy: When cleaning a room, we sometimes put items in a closet because it's the quickest and easiest way to get rid of them.

Over the years, the closet gets full. Imagine never cleaning that closet and one day opening the door to have the contents fall hard on you. You finally have to clean up. You have to sort through every single item deciding whether to keep it, throw it away, where to put it . . .in some cases you first have to identify it. My mental closet was overflowing on me. I had to address every pain I had failed to deal with for most of my young life. That, in my opinion, is the most dangerous aspect of drug abuse: losing the years of coping experience and gathering the junk I finally had to cope with. At my lowest point I was literally unable to function and seriously attempted suicide on two occasions. I need to leave that description at one sentence because to fully explain the horror show of a nightmare I went through would require another book.

The Big Point:

The worst thing drug abuse did to me was during the period in which I was drug-free.

Treatment: How to Approach Each of the Three Stages

A Word for Teachers

I've been "gung-ho" and apathetic at various times in my career. The worst thing to do is to do nothing. The flip side is, caring as much as you do, trying to help a kid who is on drugs (regardless of what stage she or he might be in) by yourself is a mistake. Teachers like to think they can handle any problem, but trying to handle this type of situation alone will lead to trouble. You might think you are helping by trying to solve the problem yourself, but more than likely you are simply prolonging the inevitable.

Parents

Dealing with a child with a drug problem can take a variety of forms especially when you take into consideration the stage he or she is in. You should not treat a Stage One abuser as you would someone who is deep into the drug culture. By doing so your efforts will most certainly do more damage than good, similar to treating the flu with chemotherapy. Keep in mind that the common thread that runs through my suggestions is communication.

As stated before, **Stage One** is the hook. Here the user is still experimenting with the drug of choice. Sending a child who's in Stage One to a treatment program is a mistake. I've seen too many kids suffer through four-week inpatient treatment programs for no reason beyond having been caught after the first time they tried marijuana. A simple talking to with some severe consequences threatened can do the trick with a Stage One user. Perhaps even a stern one-sided "contract" creating a "tight-leash" situation would be appropriate. The catch here is that you must continue to monitor your child. Adult's conversations and other resources on drug abuse aimed at teens often tend to go in one ear and out the other. Don't accept "I'll never do it again" as the end of it. Perhaps even a threat of random home urine testing will scare them away from further use. These tests can be purchased at any pharmacy but are generally not very accurate. As long as your child does not know that, the threat works.

Stage Two begins once the user is hooked and is characterized by frequent or even daily use. This is the tough one to make treatment decisions about. Do it yourself with threatened consequences, grounding, or other punishment to keep them on a tight leash, or take them straight to the treatment center. Judgment is hard to come by when dealing with an issue totally foreign to you. I wish I could give you a checklist but it's not that easy (heard that before?) Each child is a different case and to give you definitive suggestions for treatment would be irresponsible.

Stage Three is where it all begins to crash in. The user is likely getting high alone and pulling further away from human relationships. Seeking the help of a treatment center for a Stage Three abuser is recommended. Although I stopped without such measures, I endured many years of abuse before making the decision for myself. I was ready to quit. And that is a message in itself. Though your teen is this deep into abuse he or she likely has not reached the point of seeing the abuse as a problem. You will meet the most resistance from a child who is mired in Stage Three. Forcing him or her into a treatment program may be your only option and may create a huge confrontation. Understand that this type of user is likely beyond what you can do to help. Seeking the help of the police is difficult but sometimes necessary. Some treatment programs can help make it easier to get your child into treatment.

What to Look for in a Treatment Center

Some programs do too much, some do too little, and some are drastic in their measures. However, sometimes drastic measures are in order. The center I worked for as a volunteer seemed to have the right idea but executed those ideas in a robotic fashion which made their attempts ineffective. Below is a list of questions you should ask of a treatment center before making any decisions.

Do you have inpatient and outpatient services?

The best programs have both. After an evaluation, a determination is made as to where the abuser should be placed and for how long. Options are good. Inflexible programs should make you wary.

How will you determine where to place my child?

Will they treat your child like any other kid on drugs or will they meet with the child first? Do they include you in the decisions or make statements of fact without getting <u>complete</u> information from you?

What are your intake procedures?

Every program has a set, step-by-step procedure for bringing a new person into a treatment program. Ask for a copy of it; don't just let them explain it over the phone. Go over it step by step and make determinations as to whether these procedures are reasonable based on your judgment, not theirs. Intake procedures can include: a confrontation period where you air your grievances to your child and your child is not allowed to speak; an inventory-like questionnaire the teen must fill out (ask to see it); a one-on-one intake where a counselor meets with your child and discusses why he or she is there and what to expect; some programs take the teen's clothes and shoes making them earn these items back for proper response to treatment; clothes are also taken to show who's in charge or to simply avoid any potential violence or self injury. If you question any of their intake procedures, make someone at the center explain why they have adopted that particular practice.

What are the steps my child will be taken through?

Every program, regardless of being inpatient or outpatient, has different steps the patient must graduate from in order to move toward a specific goal. Is goal-setting part of the program? There should be a daily and weekly schedule that lists by hour what your child will be doing.

Get explanations about **EVERY** activity. What does it take for a child to move from step to step? How easy would it be for your child to bluff through each step?

What role do parents play in the program?

Do you have to attend counseling or group sessions with your child or other parents? Do you make decisions with the counseling staff? You should retain control of your child. A program that assumes most or the entire burden does you no good in helping your child after release from the program.

Who works there?

Ask about everyone from certified staff to volunteers. Ask to meet the people who will have contact with your teen. What are their experiences with drug abuse or counseling those who abuse drugs?

Will you provide a thorough and truthful final analysis?

Many programs do not have an out-bound procedure that is truthful in the prospects for your child's recovery. Often, teens in treatment will do whatever it takes to fake their way through a program just to get out. If the counselors can be honest and tell you the program likely failed with your child, what options do they offer?

What support does the program offer after the child leaves treatment?

What support will they offer? Will they follow up on your teen's progress? How can they help you keep your kid off drugs?

How do they respond to your questions?

Some programs will give you horror stories trying to

convince you to act immediately and admit your child. Don't let any counselor strong arm or scare you into admitting your child into a program. Other programs may be evasive because the individuals answering the phones have little to do with the overall program. Use common sense in making your decisions. If something about it seems wrong, go with your instincts even if that means looking for a treatment center 50 miles away from home.

What safety features are in place?

Sadly, sometimes during intervention teens become violent or severely depressed in response to being stuck in a rehab facility. How does the program deal with such behavior?

How do they respond to all these questions?

These questions take time to ask and answer. If the person answering these questions becomes frustrated with your extensive curiosity, then he or she does not understand your stress and concern. You must then ask yourself, how will this facility be able to understand my child's stress?

A Word about Drug Testing

I am opposed to drug testing in the workplace. I feel it is a blatant violation of an individual's Constitutional rights. However, your home is not a free society. You are responsible for your child and that gives you the right to test her or him. Home testing is not reliable and is uncomfortable for many parents. Besides, there are a variety of products on the market that help users cheat on drug tests. Methods of cheating are easier to use on a home test than those done by a clinic. The bottom line, though, is that you must take any measure you deem reasonable to protect your child.

PART 5:
THE DANGERS OF PREVENTION AND INTERVENTION TOO MUCH CARING HURTS

Has anyone ever done something because they cared about you, but that something did more damage than good? Dealing with a child who may be abusing drugs is a problem with no rules and contains traps with every decision. Careful thought about the consequences of your well-intentioned actions is impossible if you are uninformed or misinformed. This section was created out of my fear that the actions you take after reading this book might do more damage than good. Well-intentioned drug abuse programs do as much to countless kids. This is not a disclaimer, though, it is a caution. I've seen far too many parents take drastic measures with disastrous results in trying to prevent, intervene, and stop drug abuse in their teens. I've already dealt with some of these issues but I want to be clear: Any action will produce a reaction and that reaction can sometimes be more damaging than doing nothing at all.

Caution: Prevention

I remember my parents always telling me, "Don't be disappointed" if I didn't make the team, or didn't get the "A," or if something didn't work as I wanted it to. They were saying: "I care about you. I've been there. I don't want you to get hurt because failure is likely." I heard:

"You can't do it." In trying to teach coping skills we run the risk of doing more damage than good. As I said at the outset of the section on prevention, trying to control every condition that touches your child would not only be impossible but would quite likely smother your child's ability to grow as an individual. Before embracing a new attitude toward parenting, think of how those changes will be interpreted and how they will affect your child. Don't falsely prop kids up ("You can do anything") or set them up for failure ("Don't be disappointed"). Be real and honest. When teaching coping skills, understand that your child's failures are his or her best lessons. Coaching and modeling are what children need. Listen and look for how they react to your efforts.

Caution: Stopping the Abuse

Remember: panic and overreaction can be your worst enemy not only in confronting your child but also in stopping the abuse. Overreaction can push a child closer to serious drug abuse while under-reaction can let the problem slip by you. How do you measure your reaction? Use the "Three Stages of Abuse" to help determine where your child is. Treating children who are experimenting with drugs like hard-core users is overreaction. This can lead to a variety of problems including the loss of trust, feelings of betrayal, or damage done to confidence because you are subjecting them to an intense program that does not fit their abuse patterns.

Caution: Eye the "Experts" Carefully

Parents turn to so-called "experts" for help because the assumption is that they will do what's best for your child. This scares me almost as much as the abuse because of the potential damage they can do. I am not bashing all self-proclaimed teen drug abuse experts. I'm sure there are many great programs and professionals. I'm positive though that there are many poor programs and uninformed professionals. As I said in the introduction, as soon as one claims to be an expert or an authority at substance abuse treatment the claim immediately disqualifies him or her. In my opinion, no one can truly master this subject. The best anyone can claim is an understanding of the components and the complexity of substance abuse. When seeking help from drug abuse counselors, schoolteachers, school psychologists and the like, don't just listen to what they have to say. Listen and look past the words they speak to the message they are sending. Is this person a textbook professional or actually in touch with the problems children face? Trust your judgment.

A Commentary on Current Drug Prevention Practices

This book is about helping you help your child. In the process I've gotten on a variety of bandwagons and made suggestions that may seem politically charged. Perhaps. But in my years of teaching, counseling, and my years of abusing drugs I've seen dozens of attempts at prevention and intervention that do nothing but worsen the problem. For every success story, I've seen dozens of failures. The following is my way of circling the "politically motivated bandwagons" and may give you some insight to my motivations.

The Dangers of the Lie

When people care too much they can do very stupid things, which cause more problems. I taught eighth grade social studies in a Midwestern community. Drug abuse was an increasing problem at our school as it was and is at thousands of schools throughout the nation. In an attempt to do something, our administration brought in a speaker whose brother had died from an overdose of heroin. I admit upfront that I never gave this woman a chance, but due to past experience (and bias) I felt I didn't need to. I also reluctantly admit that I was being rather intellectually pompous in assuming I knew what would happen. That's another thing I don't like about experts—they do that!

After the program, one of the two counselors who sponsored the program berated me for not being at the assembly to show at least passive support for the message. I was a popular teacher at the time and the counselor feared my absence would send the wrong message to the kids who looked up to me. What would my students think I was saying by not being there? The counselor at first thought I did this out of ignorant insensitivity until I admitted that I purposely avoided the program. The shock in her face was obvious as she began to question my motives. I knew her reaction was out of sincere care for our students and I felt I owed her an explanation. I told her outright: I believe these programs do more damage than good.

Why?

Many of these "just-say-no" speakers have no idea what the drug culture is really like. Even those who have been there and are now clean buy into the "just-say-no" rhetoric in avoiding the true reasons they began abusing in the first place. The speaker who came to our school belonged to the first group. This woman's brother died from drug abuse but she was not part of it. Any message from someone who does not truly understand that culture becomes phony to kids who are in or near the culture.

Once an adult's credibility is lost, the child will shut the message out. In fact I believe it has a negative impact in that it then reinforces a kid's belief that no one really understands and that mainstream society is misinformed.

Speakers with extensive <u>knowledge</u> about drug abuse yet are lacking <u>experience</u> with it have no way of relating to those they wish to help. As an example, I may study how to be a teacher, get a doctorate in the field but without ever having actually taught I can never presume to truly understand the politics, trials, joys and frustration of teaching. I will never forget one particular session at the treatment center where I volunteered. The paid counselor on staff and I were leading a general counseling/ discussion session when one teen asked him, "Have you ever done drugs?" The answer was a reluctant "no." That was all this kid needed to hear. Slowly, every teen in the session turned the focus on how this man could not understand their unique problems. Granted, they weren't listening to what he had to say. They didn't feel they had to. He, as they saw it, could not possibly understand. This group of kids continued to use this excuse to ignore future words of wisdom from every counselor on the floor who confessed to never having "been there."

People who have never done drugs or who spew anti-drug rhetoric developed by non-users represent mainstream society (that being how we are supposed to act and look) to these kids. The mainstream is what first rejected the child who is on drugs and is thus the source and focus of his or her anger. The rejection is accompanied by negative assumptions about the mainstream as a rationalization of why they don't belong i.e. "Nobody (mainstream society) understands my problems and nobody cares to. They can't relate to my unique pain."

What's worse is when someone from the mainstream, who has not experienced the culture, attacks the drug culture and portrays it in a fictional manner. The reaction by teens who do drugs (those who are part of the drug culture) is "See, I knew it, they don't understand, that's not how people on drugs act. That's not how we are." They also see it as a person from the mainstream telling them what proper behavior is, again. Remember my cautions about what you think you know about what drugs do to people. Countless TV commercials inflate and distort the image of a person on drugs. My brain on drugs, for instance, is not a fried egg. That commercial simply scared parents and gave teens something to poke fun at.

The reaction to these distorted representations by the kids on the fringes (Stage One or curiosity) is similar and the result is worse. These kids might hangout with the drug culture kids (Stage Two and Three) in school. They see what they are like and see potential acceptance. Kids in the drug culture are "cool" because they don't seem to care about decisions of right and wrong. The pressures of youth seem to be insignificant to them. When an anti-drug speaker or advertisement displays the drug culture in a negative light by perhaps making fun of it or putting it down, the kids on the fringes instantly identify the speaker's assertion as fraudulent. The fringe kids think they know what kids who do drugs are really like. When the two descriptions (what they know versus what the speaker says) don't match, the speaker's message is lost. As an example, the speaker who came to our small Midwestern school used sauerkraut to illustrate the effects of drug abuse, slopping it in her mouth and spitting it to mimic the "idiocy" and "unattractiveness" of drug abuse. These fringe kids like the kids in the drug culture and are friends with some of them. Those drug culture kids are not unattractive and they do not seem idiotic to our fringe kids. In fact, these kids seem to be having fun while high. The portrayal doesn't match what they see. With that, the fringe kids have been given evidence supporting the drug culture's contentions that mainstream society is full of false promises and lies. That is the very reason they are on the fringe.

The Dangers of Accepting the Lie

Another danger lands on the kids who accept the message part and parcel. This is an attack from American society itself. Those kids who listen attentively to the message, agree, and then embrace the message are often embracing a half-truth. Speakers, public service announcements, and anti-drug programs often exaggerate the effects of drugs on a person. Mainstream kids accept this as truth without questioning its validity. They buy into the lies and myths without question and in a small way, their free will is damaged. If you'd rather have a child who is drug free and lacks freewill, well, we can agree to disagree. I contend we can nurture free thought and still keep our children from harmful influences without using scare tactics and lies. Remember my learned patriotism I wrote about earlier? I bought the message "our country is great" without question. Imagine again what false messages do to kids. Once that "well-adjusted" kid sees a peer on drugs not displaying the cliché portrayal shown in the message, she or he begins to question the validity of the assumption that drugs are bad. The half-truths of mainstream society suddenly revealed to the "well adjusted kid" may open new and dangerous doors to those children.

As a teen I knew a girl in high school who had bought into the message and went off to the same college I did with honors grades. Outside the influence of her "just say no" parents and friends, she met several people on drugs who did not fit the cliché description and she began experimenting. In one year's time, she went from honors student to dropout rehab patient. Kids are smart. They see that one exaggeration or lie will always be accompanied by a dozen more. When they begin to question that truth, that drugs are bad, they are lost. When they begin this questioning late in their young lives, the realization of the years of lies preceding often leads to rebellion, a reaction to feelings of betrayal.

Steven Soderbergh's movie *Traffic* (nominated for the 2000 Academy Award's best motion picture) illustrates the above point better than I. The rich kids in the movie are totally put off by the lies their parents live. They use drugs for the reasons this book discusses: because they are pressured to be perfect, because their parents are not there for them, and because they are disillusioned with the lies of mainstream society.

The Lie Incorporated:

I suppose I shouldn't be so hard on well-intentioned people and programs when their truthful aim seems to be healing and helping others. Many programs such as D.A.R.E., which is a police-led series of classroom lessons designed to teach students how to "say no" to drugs and alcohol, and A Partnership for a Drug Free America which produces several "just -say-no" public service announcements, have grown in popularity over the past decade and have impacted literally millions upon millions of children and parents worldwide. Other national, statewide and local programs based on former First Lady Nancy Reagan's "just say no" philosophy have affected countless others. When these programs first popped up I could see a shameful and hollow attempt at ending drug use among kids. It was a failure in the making which an August 2, 1999, *USA Today* article entitled "Schools' anti-drug message fails to last" confirms. D.A.R.E. is a massive and costly failure. According to the article which cites a study by the American Psychological Association,

"... more than 1,000 sixth-graders who participated in D.A.R.E., [were revisited]... 10 years later, ...[finding]: 30% used alcohol at least once a week in the past year; 46% used marijuana at least once in the past year; 24% used other drugs, such as cocaine, at least once in the past year."

Further, an August 1999 article in the *Journal of Consulting and Clinical Psychology* entitled "D.A.R.E.: No Effects at 10-Year Follow-Up" states: "Consistent with other scientifically sound studies, we found that D.A.R.E. had no effect on students' drug use at any time through 10th grade... At age 20, there were no differences between those who received D.A.R.E. and those who did not in their use of alcohol, other drugs, etc."

Countless more research studies arrived at the same conclusions. Though D.A.R.E. would argue that drug use among teens has dropped overall since the 1980's they cannot make an effective claim that they or other programs actually played a part in this reduction. Beyond the statistical failure, I apply my previous arguments about the damage such misinformed preventative measures can do to children. Programs such as these have institutionalized the lies about drug abuse and have likely (though I have no evidence) done great damage to our society.

In addition, one must question an obvious ambiguity perpetuated by proponents of such programs. If drug abuse is indeed a disease, why are we sending thousands of people suffering from this "disease" to prison? Why are we as a nation allowing billions of dollars to be spent on locking up the drug problem rather than resolving it? Why isn't A Partnership for a Drug Free America (which spends millions on anti-drug advertising) attacking teen alcohol abuse (which as previously stated is far more deadly to teens) with the veracity they do illicit drugs? Why isn't there a "War on Alcohol"? Legality has nothing to do with abuse tendencies.

I can not outright claim nor suggest there is a covert agenda for bilking the American people out of billions of dollars for "prevention (lies) and treatment (jail)" but I could certainly find far more productive ways to spend D.A.R.E.'s 220 million dollar annual budget or countless state budgets dedicated to sending drug users to prison.

To Their Wits' End

My parents never acknowledged my drug abuse. I do not know if they were oblivious or they just did not want to know. They only responded to my increasing anti-social behavior, which was a result of my inability to cope with living. As a teen I didn't like them very much, and I don't think they liked me either—as hard as they tried. That's not to say they did not love or care about me. They had come to their wits' end. I was rebellious, defiant, cold, mean, and unwilling to show any effort to make anything of myself. Our shouting matches had turned into a cold war of non-communication. I wouldn't allow discussion nor any effort they put forth to break the silence. By the time I had graduated from high school, they had all but given up on me. But they still had hope. Why? I have no idea; perhaps it was the blind love a parent feels for a child. Keep in mind, though, that by this time, many of my drug friends' parents had completely given up on them.

Many were kicked out of their homes by the age of 17. Others were allowed to live in the family's basement as long as they did not bother their parents. Some just faded away. A few died or were sent to prison. My parents' best hopes for me were that I'd pick up a useful trade and become productive in some manner. I had given them no reason to believe that I would. I did my best to prove that I was a failure while secretly holding onto the hope that I wasn't. I did not let them know who I was. I did not share those hopes. The more involved in the drug culture I got, the less cooperative, less caring, and less willing to be their child I became. I indeed had turned into a bad kid.

My parents did not kick me out of the house—a fact that still amazes me considering some of the stunts I pulled. They continued to care. It was that lone effort, that basic message of "we still care" that made the difference. After I received an invitation and a financial grant to attend the state university, my parents agreed to pay for a portion of my first two years of college. Out of hope, desperation, and caring, they took a risk on a bet they had no reason to believe they'd win. They gave me the means to succeed—the basic necessities to live and survive in a college setting—but I had to take those means and produce. They could do nothing to effect that. I had to take responsibility for my life. After doing well my first year (due to studying a subject I loved), hope shone through and gave them enough confidence in my progress to financially assist me for two more years of college. I had friends who were in a similar situation where Mom and Dad paid for everything that first year of college only to see their son or daughter waste the money and flunk out. This was not the case for me. I was holding down a good part-time job and proved that I was willing to help myself. I showed them a little effort and they showed increasing confidence.

Long story short. I've let go of most of the demons of the past, and now have a good adult relationship with "Ma and Pop" as I call them. We lost a lot of time that cannot be made up but we have forgiven each other for the mistakes we made. I love them and care for them deeply. They are proud of me today and that means the world to me. It was the fact that they never fully gave-up on me that gave me the means to succeed. Without the opportunities college gave me I would likely be in a very dark place right now.

Don't give up on your child. No matter what, you must support them to the end, whether they make it or not. And I will be honest; some don't make it. I was lucky. And without elaborating further, I still fight my abusive tendencies and a few of those demons of the past but as of today, I am happy, free, and confident, and those are great feelings.

A Final Word

I've been ambiguous at just about every corner and with many assertions I've made—for a reason. I believe strongly in everything I have said. Why didn't I just say that from the start instead of seemingly sitting on the fence? Two reasons. One, I am not an expert. Despite my opinion of experts, for me to tell you to ignore them would be irresponsible. For me to urge you toward any one belief or action would be hypocritical. You must make these decisions on your own based on your unique situation. Two, in this text I often talked of building confidence in your child. You must possess that confidence first. If I played the role of expert you might have gotten a burst of that confidence and dove head long into the problem. But that confidence would be based on inspiration and inspired confidence fades with the slightest of doubts. Your confidence in dealing with your child's problems must be real and unwavering.

The Final Point:

Educate yourself in order to educate your children. Trust your decisions, acknowledge your mistakes, and be honest with yourself and your teen. Be strong and stay strong, for strength is a potent ally. And finally, true confidence in yourself and your abilities as a parent will work wonders. That confidence won't let you give up.

Resources Provided by the Department of Education, USA

Treatment Referral: Help in Finding Treatment Centers

American Council for Drug Education
Information: 800-488-DRUG, www.acde.org
Referrals: 800-DRUG HEL(P), www.drughelp.org

National Council on Alcoholism and Drug Dependence, Inc.
12W. 21st Street, 7th Floor
New York, NY 10010
800-NCA-CALL
www.ncadd.org

Substance Abuse and Mental Health Services/Center for Substance Abuse Treatment
Department of Health and Human Services (Provides counseling referrals by state)
NCADI
P.O. Box 2345
Rockville, MD 20847-2345
800-662-HELP
www.drughelp.org

For Families:

Families Anonymous, Inc
(Offers a 12 step program to help families of former or current, or suspected drug abusers.)
P.O. Box 3475
Culver City, CA 90231-3475
800-736-9805

Mothers Against Drunk Driving, MADD
511 E. John Carpenter Freeway, Suite 700
Irving, TX 75062
800-GET MADD
www.madd.org

General Information:

National Institute on Drug Abuse (NIDA)
(Provides an estimated 85% of the world's research and study of drug abuse.)
5600 Fishers Lane, Rockville MD 20857
301-443-1124
www.nida.nih.gov

Parents and Adolescents Recovering Together Successfully (PARTS)
A self-help group supporting families in recovery
12815 Stebick Court
San Diego, CA 92310-2705
619-698-3449

Partnership for a Drug Free America
(Produces public service announcements and anti-drug messages. They also operate a detailed website which is a good resource for researching substances not detailed in

this book.)
405 Lexington Ave, Suite 1601
New York, NY 10174
212-922-1560
www.drugfreeamerica.org

About the Author:

Alan Sharpe, author of *Drugs, Lies & Teenagers,* is a 12th grade social studies teacher in Compton, California. He has also taught 8th grade Social Studies in Pekin, Illinois. He has an MA in Educational Technology from Pepperdine University as well as a BA in History Education from Illinois State University.